AGAINST REFORM

In *Against Reform*, John Pepall offers a stringent critique of proposed reforms to Canada's political institutions. Examining electoral reform, an elected or provincially appointed Senate and reduced terms for senators, fixed election dates, recall, initiative, and parliamentary reform, including 'free votes' and parliamentary confirmation of appointments, Pepall contends that these reforms are ill-conceived and would be harmful.

At the root of Pepall's critique is an argument that, in Canada today, too many voters are quick to blame institutions rather than their own conflicting interests and understandings when they do not receive what they want out of government. While considering influential factors such as academic and media bias, political fashion, and the American example, Pepall's unique and highly readable assessment takes aim at the practical and theoretical understandings of reform across party lines.

(University of Toronto Centre for Public Management Monograph Series on Public Policy and Public Administration)

JOHN PEPALL is a writer and political commentator based in Toronto.

The University of Toronto Centre for Public Management Monograph Series

Editor: Andrew Stark, University of Toronto
Funder: The Donner Canadian Foundation

The University of Toronto Centre for Public Management Monograph Series is an ongoing series of books on important topical matters in public administration and public policy that will engage not only the academic community but also policy- and opinion-makers in Canada and elsewhere.

Books are included in the series based on their originality, capacity to provoke public debate, and academic rigour.

For a list of books published in the series, see page 165.

JOHN PEPALL

Against Reform

University of Toronto Centre for Public Management Monograph Series

© University of Toronto Press Incorporated 2010
Toronto Buffalo London
www.utppublishing.com
Printed in Canada

ISBN 978-0-7727-8624-1 (cloth)
ISBN 978-0-7727-8623-4 (paper)

Printed on acid-free, 100% post-consumer recycled paper with
vegetable-based inks.

Library and Archives Canada Cataloguing in Publication

Pepall, John, 1949–
Against reform / John Pepall.

(University of Toronto Centre for Public Mgmt monograph series)
Includes bibliographical references and index.
ISBN 978-0-7727-8624-1 (bound). – ISBN 978-0-7727-8623-4 (pbk.)

1. Canada – Politics and government – 1993–2006.   2. Canada – Politics
and government – 2006– .   I. Title.   II. Series: University of Toronto
Centre for Public Management monograph series

JL86.P64P46 2010   320.971'09051   C2010-905024-X

Produced for the University of Toronto Centre for Public Management by the
University of Toronto Press.

For Mitzi

Contents

Foreword

The Canadian political system, with its unique array of discontents, has long nurtured a corresponding set of reform proposals. At any given time some have figured more prominently than others, although in the past two decades all of them have reached what passes in Canada for fever pitch. Proposals for electoral reform, Senate reform, fixed election dates, parliamentary review of judicial appointments, recall, referenda, and changes to party discipline in the House of Commons have all been in the news of late. And whatever they are, John Pepall's against them.

Until Pepall's book, no one had looked at all these ideas in tandem, much less done so in such a compelling and provocative way. By bringing all these reform proposals together and then taking such a clear stand, Pepall is sure to stir debate. The book is a rarity – a polemic in the best sense that's rooted in a deep reading of the literature and an understanding of the country and its traditions.

Pepall takes a conservative stance on the issues he examines, but not in a partisan way. Ideas associated with Stephen Harper and the Conservative Party come in for their share of criticism, as do those linked with nearly every other party and faction in the country. What's most deeply conservative about his approach, though, is that it's animated by no overarching theory or vision. Instead, for each reform idea, Pepall fashions bespoke critiques, confronting it with its own particular problems and contradictions, and in the process making insightful arguments that are wholly original, both in academic and broader public terms.

William F. Buckley once identified his brand of conservatism with the idea that 'I would rather be governed by the first 2000 names in the Boston phone book than by the 2000 members of the faculty of Harvard University.' Pepall, I think it's safe to say, would be equally cool to either option. Part of his opposition to the reforms he considers stems from a sense that no matter how smart a professor – or politician – may be, whatever reform he proposes is bound to contain more hidden discontents than the way things are at the moment. Another part of Pepall's resistance to reform stems from a conviction that the citizenry is best served by the broad-brush democracy we now have – we review the government record on an as-needed basis at the polls and say yea or nay – and that any institutional alterations meant to more continually and deeply engage, monitor, mirror, or take the pulse of public opinion are bound to lead to trouble down the road.

Better, then, that we leave well enough alone. I am pleased to have the opportunity – and grateful, as always, to the Donner Canadian Foundation for providing the means – to publish this timely, innovative, and beautifully crafted book in the University of Toronto Centre for Public Management Monograph Series.

Andrew Stark
Editor
University of Toronto Centre for Public Management Monograph Series

Acknowledgments

The arguments of this book intervene in the public discussion of its several subjects in the media and politics. I have researched the academic and historical literature. All this appears in the notes.

But I want to acknowledge the help of Richard Lubbock, broadcaster, journalist, and curious citizen, who first put me onto the paradox of voting, Condorcet, Arrow etc.; H. Donald Forbes of the Department of Political Science at the University of Toronto, with whom I had fruitful discussions as the work progressed; and poet, lexicographer, and editor Fraser Sutherland, who gave me stern advice and encouragement.

AGAINST REFORM

1 Introduction

This book attacks each of the several radical changes to our political institutions and procedures that have, under the name of reform, been promoted in Canada in the last two decades. Some have already been adopted and several are on the national or provincial agenda. Fixed election dates have been adopted in Ottawa and seven provinces and one territory. We have had our first judge hauled before members of Parliament before ascending to the Supreme Court. Recall and Initiative legislation was passed in British Columbia in 1995. Senators may be about to be elected, sort of. In several provinces electoral reform has been proposed, and there have been four referendums on it.

Each reform is fuelled by particular pressures and misunderstandings and presents particular dangers. I deal with each briefly or at length, as its importance and complexities indicate. But though each stands or falls on its own, has its particular proponents, and may, both in theory and in practice, conflict with others, powerful common influences propel them forward.

We have forgotten how and why our political institutions came to be. The media, academics, and politicians have a bias towards change, and the mass of people who are content with our institutions are quiet, while those keen on change will not be quiet. We are distracted by the spectacle of American politics. Most importantly we misunderstand democracy and, in the hope of getting what we think the people want, risk the people losing control of government.

Oblivion

Decade after decade, elections were held, governments were formed, went about their business, and fell, under the rules and conventions that are now almost all under attack. There were great political controversies, wars and depressions, conflicts within the country, but claims that our political institutions were flawed were not heard. Vast material and arguable social progress took place. There was a general belief that we had happily inherited and developed sound institutions. We ought not lightly to put aside what was so long thought to work well. But a century and more of content with our political institutions is forgotten in the general oblivion of Canada's past.

Behind Canada's experience with our existing political institutions lie centuries of political evolution in Britain. Very little of this was the result of conscious political theory. By a process of trial and error, institutions were developed that provided effective government answerable to the people. Two generations ago that history and the achievements of the governments it led to were well known in Canada. They too have passed into oblivion.

It was once understood that our political institutions were a primary part of who we are and an object of pride. In the remaking of Canada, at once aggressive and surreptitious, in the last forty years this understanding has been suppressed. How and why our existing institutions came to be and why thoughtful people in the past defended them is hardly taught in schools and universities.

When the issue of confidence is raised in the House of Commons[1] it is treated as if it arose from some arcane rule, perhaps medieval, as most things old and not understood are supposed to be. In fact it is perfectly simple and practical. We must have a government, and that government, to govern, must generally be able get its measures, particularly its financial measures, through the House of Commons. It is through the popularly elected House of Commons that practically we choose our government. But the Commons in choosing a government assumes a responsibility to support it, to give it its confidence. If it will not support it, it must either find and support another government in the existing House or be dissolved so that another House of Commons can be elected that will support a government.

Whether a government has the confidence of the Commons is a matter of judgment, easy enough in most cases, when a confidence motion has been won or lost, but not requiring experts to decide, even when it is difficult. It is only because a basic understanding of how our institutions work, and they do work, has been lost that something so simple can seem technical.

With all understanding of our political institutions, and all confidence in and respect for our past gone, our political institutions become vulnerable to any novelty. The constitutional wrangling of the 1980s, whose object was to resolve the problem of Quebec, opened arguments about the Senate and the Supreme Court. They led to nothing. Exhaustion put the constitution off the political agenda for the foreseeable future. But a taste for tinkering with our political institutions remained.

Professional Bias

There is a journalistic bias towards reform. Calls for reform of our political institutions are a staple of the comment pages in the newspapers. Editors like an argument that something is wrong and changes are needed. Every time there has been a Supreme Court vacancy, and often when there has not, articles have been printed calling for some kind of parliamentary confirmation of judicial appointments. Some law professors have got to make the same argument several times. An argument that all is well and no change is needed does not seem to merit space. Only after several arguments for reform have appeared is an argument against reform admitted as a novelty.

The reform bug has passed on to editorial boards, and many newspapers have added their solemn voices to the call for reform. This done, they are even less likely to admit an argument against reform, and academic studies or news releases calling for reform are readily printed.

Polls show broad support for all kinds of reform. Only rarely are reforms criticized. While on all the substantive issues of politics – taxes, health, education, crime, war and peace – there is controversy, division between and within parties, heat if not light, on reform all is quiet. Some advocates of reform are full of passionate intensity and foresee the dawning of a new age when their reforms are adopted. But the mass of people who tell pollsters that they want reform, or who voted for the single transferable vote (STV) in the first British Columbia referendum, hardly seem excited by the prospect. Much reform electoral reform particularly – is highly technical, an added delight to its obsessive advocates. The broad public who say they want it do not give it much thought. They suppose 'reform' is obviously improvement. Those who do not support reform are equally passionless. They are content to leave well enough alone. Calls for reform are to them a distraction from substantive issues. In this climate, arguments for reform advance by default.

Politicians too have a professional bias towards reform. A popular suspicion that politicians cling to the status quo out of self-interest, that they constitute the principal barrier to a brave new world of reform, is sadly groundless. Politicians in all parties, hoping to seem high-minded and thoughtful, and pandering to the polls, advocate some or all of the reforms that I attack in this book. Politicians love a new idea, regardless of its worth. It gets them attention. It gives them something to talk about and perhaps something to do. Political reform, like foreign travel, makes a welcome break from the usual stuff of politics. It seems grand, high-minded, above the partisan fray. No one's taxes will be raised by it, no debt incurred. It requires no spending that may go awry, no intrusion of government into people's lives. So it seems. As it makes government incompetent, all this may follow. But those who call for reform see no farther into the future than they do into the past.

Political scientists suffer from the usual deformation of the modern academic: always wanting to have a better idea to justify their existence. A prejudice against what is old is reinforced by experts with an interest in novelty.

In fact none of the proposed reforms are new. Proportional representation and other electoral systems were first proposed in the nineteenth century and adopted in several European countries as democracy took hold. Recall and initiative are also nineteenth-century inventions adopted variously in Switzerland, the United States, and elsewhere. But until recent years there was no significant movement for reform in Canada.[2] A very few academics, when there were far fewer academics than there are now, and a few cranks wrote about such things, but little attention was paid to them.

Yankee Do

Many proposed reforms are based on or influenced by American models: a triple-E Senate, parliamentary confirmation of judicial and other appointments, fixed terms, 'free votes' and associated parliamentary reforms, recall, initiative. It is not an argument against a reform to say that it apes American institutions and practices. It is no more an argument for a reform to say that the Americans do it that way. But it is an inescapable fact that many Canadians, as much those who denounce American policies and cry for independence and for protection from American culture as any, are mesmerized by the spectacle of American politics. American prestige and self-confidence draw many unthinking to their institutions.

We should reject American models for three reasons. First, because responsible parliamentary government is better than congressional government and separation of powers. Woodrow Wilson, for one, thought so.[3] Second, you cannot pick and choose elements from one system or another. With all its faults, American government was conceived as a whole with its checks and balances. You cannot safely take two checks and one balance from it and leave the rest. If you like the United States Constitution, you must take it whole, as the annexationists of the 1850s would have. Finally, the Americans make their institutions work, more or less, because of a complex adaptation of their political culture to them. What may, just, work in the United States political culture will not work here.

Misunderstanding Democracy

Reform is often called democratic reform. Democracy is an unquestioned faith. That it should be our faith is good. That it should be unquestioned is not – not because democracy is not a good thing, but because unquestioned it is not understood.

The popular understanding of democracy is that it assures that we get in government what the people want. It is accepted that this may not always be for the best: 'People get the government they deserve.' But at least if they get what they want, people will be content until experience illumined by free debate teaches them that they can do better.

At the root of the discontent that fuels the reform agenda is a feeling that we are not getting the government we deserve, that our institutions do not give us what the people want. Reformers do not understand the confusion concealed in the phrase *what the people want*. It is generally understood that *people* must mean 'a majority of people.' It is not generally understood how seldom a majority can be found for the choices that must and will be made across the broad field of people and policies that is government, whether or not there is a majority.

This is partly revealed by polls. People responding to polls can be incoherent. Majorities can easily be elicited in favour of inconsistent policies: lower taxes, higher spending, and declining debt. A slight shift in the wording of questions can elicit majorities for or against the CBC or private health care. People responding to polls are not making decisions that they must live with and answer for. They are giving an opinion, often on subjects they have scarcely thought about, and when they might more accurately have answered that they had no opinion. And opinions can swing widely in short periods of time: on having our forces in Afghanistan or gay marriage as well as party preferences and politician approval.

Public opinion or what the people want can safely be incoherent or swing this way and that. Government cannot. It must stick to its choices and take responsibility for them. 'To govern is to choose.' Any form of government will make the choices of which government consists. Even a government paralyzed by conflict, incoherence, and confusion will make those choices, if only by default. The people as a whole will not understand many of the choices, will have no opinion on many, will not even know that some are being made.

There is no escaping government. Big or small and of whatever hue, it will always be with us. In governing it will make myriad decisions, and many of these will not be what a majority of people want, because there is no majority for one choice rather than another. And governments cannot cut taxes, raise spending, and reduce debt. They must decide where the people are undecided.

So democracy cannot always give the people what they want. It can only make government answerable to the people for what it does. So long as people wrongly think government can give them what they want, they will pursue futile and harmful efforts at reform.

What Everybody Thinks

Many people make the mistake of thinking that what they want is what most people want. People usually spend most of their time with like-minded people. They read a newspaper or listen to a radio station that sees things much as they do. There are marked regional variations in public opinion, and people in one region will feel that what is prevailing opinion in their region is, or should be, prevailing opinion everywhere. They come to think that most people think as they do. When governments do not do what prevailing opinion, as they perceive it, demands, they think there must be something wrong.

They are ready for the reform agenda. They think that the way to get what they want in government is to change political institutions rather than to persuade those they wrongly take to be an interested minority to come round to their way of thinking, or, perhaps, to change their thinking by listening to other opinions.

This mistake has been encouraged by Canada's regional divisions. In the last three decades of the twentieth century there was a persistent and well-grounded feeling in Western Canada that anxiety over Quebec separatism and the sheer weight of Ontario's population and economy was leading to a neglect of the West by Ottawa. This alienation led to reform ideas finding a Canadian home in a West with a culture already more open to American influence and with a history of successful populist movements. The Reform Party, though perceived as a conservative party, under Preston Manning's leadership put an elected Senate and parliamentary reform on the agenda. In part Westerners simply wanted more power for the West, something the growing population of the West was bringing them anyway. But in part Westerners supposed that what they thought was what most people thought but could not make effective because of what was called a 'democratic deficit.'

It is a usual claim of reformers that people have lost faith in politicians, and reforms are needed to restore faith. They do no say how once our unreformed institutions produced politicians who were trusted. The claim of lost faith is groundless. As long as there have been politicians, they have been mistrusted. Only ignorance of history and a factitious nostalgia could make anyone think otherwise. Though, when partisanship and sectarian and other interests were stronger, people may have thought that *their* politicians could be trusted and the other ones were no worse than the rabble they represented.

The increased weight and intrusiveness of government, while it has led some to call for less government, invigorating the right for a time, led more generally to a wish to control it. In a bigger and more diverse population, people felt less close to politicians. Better communications and television do not bridge the gap. They impress on people the remoteness of those who govern them.

In the past, people thought the problem was the other guys: the Tories thought it was the Grits; the Grits the Tories. They knew them. Now it is all strangers on TV.

Some readers may think that I believe all is for the best in the best of all possible worlds, that because I think our institutions are sound and should not be messed about, I think that our politics are wonderful and our politicians are doing a wonderful job. I do not. I hope at another time to set out what I think is wrong with our politics. A lot. But the fixation with reform and the delusion that, with reform, all will be well in our politics prevents us from seeing what is wrong. The fault is not in our institutions that we are ill served.

I prefer the distillation of experience in our existing political institutions to whatever the politicians of today can come up with. I am consistent in thinking our institutions are sound and our politicians are not because our institutions were not made by our politicians.

2 If It Ain't Broke, Fix It: Fixed Election Dates

With much self-congratulation, fixed election dates, often, significantly, called fixed terms, have already been adopted in seven provinces and the Northwest Territories, and, on the initiative of the Harper government, in Ottawa. After British Columbia led the way in 2001, other jurisdictions fell like dominoes to this most fashionable of reforms. In Alberta a Tory's private member's bill has been sidelined, and in Nova Scotia a private member's bill introduced by the now leader of the Liberal opposition never came to a vote. Quebec has other things on its mind. But the tide seems irresistible.

It seems a slight, sensible thing, though extravagant claims are made for it. Why should we not know when the next election will be?

Fixed-term legislation attempts to fix the date of future elections in advance. The dates of the British Columbia elections of 17 May 2005 and 12 May 2009 were fixed by statute, and future elections are supposed to be held every four years on the second Tuesday in May. The Harper government's bill, passed in May 2007, set 19 October 2009 as the date for the next election, and thereafter the third Monday in October every four years, though thereon hangs a tale.

It is not so simple and easy as to most people it seems. Ontario settled on 4 October 2007, four years after the election that brought Dalton McGuinty's Liberals to power, but with eight months to go had to shift to 10 October because of a Jewish holiday. Such inconveniences are only the tip of the iceberg, usually anticipated in the legislation.

If fixed election dates are such a no-brainer, at worst harmless, how is it that we did without them for so long and so many parliamentary democracies still do. Are we experiencing a sudden access of intelligence and integrity, led by the vast majority of the political establishment of whom reformers are so suspicious, at the dawn of the twenty-first century?

The phrase *fixed terms* – the Ontario legislation speaks of 'four-year terms' – reveals a confusion on which the reform is partly based. American federal and state constitutions prescribe fixed terms for their politicians. Our politicians do not have terms. Ministers and parliamentary secretaries or assistants serve in government 'at pleasure,' in practice so long as the prime minister or premier chooses. Prime ministers or premiers serve as long as the House of Commons or the legislative assembly will support a government they lead. MPs and MLAs serve as long as Parliament or the legislative assembly lasts. Parliament and legislative assemblies last as long as a government commanding a majority chooses or until no government can be formed with the House made up as it is. Americans are stuck with their politicians for however long their terms may be. Our politicians serve as long as they can work together effectively, for good or ill.

Broadly speaking there are two kinds of democratic government: congressional government modelled on what the United States devised after the American Revolution with fixed terms and separation of powers between the executive and the legislature, and parliamentary government inspired by what had evolved in Britain by the early nineteenth century. Under congressional government Congress can do a lot, whether the president likes it or not, and the president can do a lot, whether Congress likes it or not. They can stop each other from doing some things but cannot make each other do anything. It is best that they cooperate, but Congress can still legislate and the president execute up to a point, even if they do not. They are separate powers. In parliamentary government the government is drawn from and depends on the support of the legislature and can do nothing without the support of the legislature. Power is not separated but entwined, and the government and the legislature must work together. That is why, whatever the restrictions, which can usually be overcome, parliamentary governments do not have fixed terms, while congressional governments do. The attempt to fix election dates in Canada without frankly throwing over parliamentary government and going American only creates confusion and trouble.

The parliamentary governments that have the most restrictions on election dates have proportional representation. The reason for this, as will appear later, is that elections make much less difference under proportional representation. The government may change several times between elections, and the shifts in party strength after an election may do nothing to resolve a parliamentary impasse.

Parliament and the legislative assemblies already have a limit set to their lives – generally five years – but it is not a fixed term. This was the fruit of hundreds of years of contest and evolution. Kings originally summoned parliaments when they wanted and for as long as they wanted. From the seventeenth century there was a clamour for triennial parliaments, and, for much of the eighteenth and nineteenth centuries, parliaments could last for as long as seven years. Everyone seems to have been content when five years was generally settled on for the life of a parliament. For all the insistence that the people must have their say, elections are generally unpopular and voters prefer not to be bothered with them more often than necessary. The fixed-term legislation in the provinces and Ottawa provides for elections every four years, practically shortening the lives of Parliaments and legislative assemblies, but it was not for that purpose that it was promoted.

The Progressive Conservatives in Ottawa in 1993 and the New Democrats in Ontario in 1995, facing certain defeat, held on to almost the end of the five-year life of Parliament, but generally governments have called elections in the first half of the fifth year after the last election. Various conveniences have been considered in choosing a date for general elections, but generally the timing of elections has not been controversial. The proponents of fixed terms speak glowingly about their reform and scathingly of the status quo: 'a Premier sitting back and picking the election date based on what the oracles in the Premier's office and the party office have to say about when an election has to be held.'[4] Elections, they say, 'do not belong to Premiers to use as they see fit for their own political agenda.'[5]

Most people tell pollsters they think fixed terms are a good idea. But generally, as elections have been called, there has been no complaint about the timing, or only vague grumbling that was as much about the annoyance and expense of an election that seemed to have been called early, as any suspicion of abuse of an arbitrary power.

The fixing of election dates in advance by law is intended to solve a problem that does not exist. When the government party has a secure majority, it is free to ask for a dissolution and a general election whenever it wants to. As there can be no question of another party or parties forming a government in the existing house, the governor general or lieutenant governor is bound to agree. The problem alleged is that the government party could use its power to choose the date of the election for political advantage, choosing a moment when it stood well in the polls, for what might be passing reasons, to secure another majority, or at least a gentler defeat, than its record on a fixed election date might have yielded.

There has been no occasion when a government actually managed to pull a fast one, as it were, on the electorate, catching it in a mellow mood and getting re-elected, when at a fixed date, a few months earlier or later, the voters would have rejected it. If political strategists think they can do it, more fools they. It is laughable that it should have been a Liberal government in Ontario that introduced fixed terms, having promised to in the 2003 election. The one time an Ontario government did try to exploit its power to call an election when it wished was when the previous Liberal government of Ontario under David Peterson called an election for September 1990 only thirty-nine months after the last election and when it had twenty months before it had to. The Liberals stood high in the polls. They suffered a crushing defeat and spent thirteen years in opposition.

It is impossible that a government could decide on an election date on the basis of partisan political calculations without the opposition and the press being aware of them and free to make them an issue. The sanction that prevents governments from abusing the power to pick election dates is the judgment of the people on the appointed day. If the government tries to pull a fast one, it will suffer, as Peterson found.

The premise of fixed-date proponents is that governments can take advantage of passing strength in the polls by calling a 'snap' election. But passing strength in the polls, by its very nature, cannot be caught in a snap election. If it is passing, it may well pass in the weeks between the calling of an election and the voting. The calling of an election, and the focusing of voters' minds on the coming decision, generally makes a significant difference to the polls anyway. On the other hand, if a government's strength in the polls is sustained, partisan political considerations cannot enter into election timing.

If governments were so free as is alleged to exploit their power to call elections when they see fit for partisan advantage, they would call elections after less than a year in office, when they often enjoy a honeymoon with the voters. But they know that they would suffer if they did. In practice, the freedom that majority governments have to choose an election date is simply a flexibility in the last third of the five-year life of Parliament.

In choosing election dates, governments may seek advantage from being sensitive to the weather and what the voters are up to, getting what they want done in Parliament, without railroading, or the appeal of new measures to be promoted in an election. But these are only partisan motives so far as they please the voters. That can hardly be an objection. Of course they want to win. But after four years in office a government is either going to win on its record and what the opposition is offering or it is not. It cannot place its hopes on catching a wave in the polls.

It may be a shabby thing to pick an election date for partisan reasons. As the Peterson example shows, governments will suffer if they do it. But objecting to choosing an election date for partisan reasons implies that there are right reasons for choosing and a right date. There is no reason why the right date should be, as near as the calendar permits, exactly four years after the last election. When to call an election is a matter of judgment, like most of what governments do. We cannot forbid governments to make decisions. We can only judge them at the polls, as Ontario did Peterson.

Much of what modern governments do, and opposition parties propose, is calculated for electoral advantage. Governments cut taxes and spend money to assure their re-election. The opposition tries to outbid them without counting the cost. We cannot forbid governments to cut taxes or spend money because they may do it for the wrong reasons. We must simply judge them, and their opponents. If we judge them wisely, what they do for partisan advantage rather than the common weal will redound against them. It is up to us.

Jean Chrétien enjoyed winning elections and called them roughly every three and a half years. Perhaps he had hoped to fit in another in June 2004. But there can be no question that he would have won as handily if forced to keep to a four-year schedule. If people did not like him calling elections a bit early, they could have shown it by voting for one of the remarkable array of opposition parties available. But they were in the main content to confirm what they had said in the last election. It was alleged by some that he called the election of November 2000 to wrong-foot the Canadian Alliance under its new leader Stockwell Day. The disarray in the opposition in those years was such that there was never a time when such an allegation could not have been made. He could hardly have been asked to wait for them to sort themselves out, to make the advantage of the opposition the standard of election timing.

If fault there was in Chrétien's fondness for elections, it was the opposite of what fixed-term proponents claim. Chrétien was not concerned to catch passing strength in the polls. He was using his sustained strength to notch up victories he could have at will.

On the other hand, why should Paul Martin have been forced to wait out a four-year term on succeeding Chrétien before seeking his own victory? The succession of a new leader of a governing party as prime minister is the most obvious occasion on which there is often an argument that there should be an early election. It seems likely that on such occasions, and perhaps others, governments may seek to free themselves from the straitjacket of fixed election dates. They may be pressed to do so. But the legislation, though easily got round, in fact not binding at all as we have learned, presents a distracting argument, should governments, however rightly, do so.

Some enthusiasts for reform, being of a wonky bent, will see every objection only as an occasion for the development of ingenious new rules. So it might be proposed that the succession of a new leader of the governing party should trigger an election out of the fixed schedule. Newfoundland and Labrador has done just that in providing that, if there is a new premier less than three years after an election, he or she must advise the lieutenant governor to dissolve the house of assembly and call an election within twelve months.[6]

But something can be a good reason for doing something without it necessitating or justifying a rule requiring it. If every change of a governing party's leader forced an election, it would create a dangerous barrier against challenging a leader. Rebels against a failing leader would be inhibited and the leader's position strengthened – something reformers say they are against. In any event, sometimes the argument that a new leader should have time to build up a record in office is persuasive. The long-anticipated succession of Gordon Brown to Tony Blair in Britain, about two years after the last election and two years before the next was anticipated, did not entail an election. Voters may want to size up a new prime minister before voting. It is a matter of judgment. Finally the voters will judge.

The Conservative opposition leader David Cameron taunted Brown to call an election. To his chagrin there was a 'Brown bounce' in the polls. When election dates are not fixed, opposition parties can challenge the government to call an election – a perfectly legitimate political stand that is taken from the opposition when election dates are fixed. It was a turning point for Brown when he showed he did not have the 'bottle' to call an election he might have won handily.

The politicians introducing fixed-term legislation spoke conceitedly of a kind of new dawn for democracy and claimed that fixed terms would restore public trust in politicians. But whatever reasons people may have for not trusting politicians, there was never any evidence that the timing of elections was one of them, until reformers proclaimed that politicians could not be trusted to pick election dates. The reformers created the mistrust they purported to dispel. Though large majorities tell pollsters that they support fixed election dates, it cannot be pretended that they were brought in by popular demand. They had support, sadly, in all parties and were little debated.

The seed of fixed terms was not public mistrust of politicians but sore losers. Politicians are reluctant to accept that they lose elections through their own faults, by failing to persuade voters. They prefer to tell themselves and the media that some shoddy gambit of their opponents led to their defeat. If only the election had been a little sooner, or later, they would have won.

The keenness with which politicians, particularly governing politicians, have embraced the fixed-date fad should give pause to voters who support it on the cynical suspicion that the power to choose election dates gives governments an unfair advantage. Do politicians understand something the voters don't, that there is no partisan advantage in the power to pick election dates? Perhaps the opposite.

Voters who tell pollsters that it is unfair that governments should have the power to call elections may be expressing their annoyance at being bothered with elections in what they think is a respectable way. It wouldn't do to say they don't like elections. So they say elections are called unfairly. Premiers bringing in fixed election dates give up no advantage and wash their hands of responsibility for calling elections. They are safe from public annoyance at being bothered with an election because the wonderful new law, they can say, gives them no choice.

People expect a lot from government but, encouraged by reformers to be suspicious, they resent governments actually exercising power. Many reforms aim to limit the ability of governments to act. Politicians are happier with this than most people imagine, often being interested not so much in the power of government as in the status and celebrity of office. The proffered solution to the false problem of election timing is to remove all power and discretion and fix election dates arbitrarily.

A trivial argument – that fixed dates would be more convenient for election officials, and even party officials – is made. But unless we are to adopt the United States Constitution and congressional government, there will always be the possibility of elections brought on by the fall of a minority government, and officials will have to be ready. And by-elections may be necessary anywhere, any time. Election officials like fixed election dates because it makes their lives easier. If election officials come to expect easy lives and are not ready for unscheduled elections, that is another harm in the legislation.

What flexibility the legislation provides to accommodate religious holidays or elections at other levels of government it generally puts in the hands of election officials. If anyone is going to pick election dates, it should be responsible politicians and not officious bureaucrats. Elections Alberta strongly recommended fixed election dates in its report after the 2008 election in that province.[7] The self-righteous impertinence of independent government bodies promoting legislation and even constitutional changes to make their work easier and their power greater is a constant menace to good government.

The Downside

Fixed election dates repair no fault because none existed. They bring their own problems. Instead of governments slyly trying to time elections for their advantage, which they could never do, they will try to time their measures to put voters in a good mood on the fixed date. Tax cuts and bountiful spending and cheering initiatives will be delayed or brought forward for maximum impact on the appointed day. As happens in the United States, electioneering will extend months and even years ahead of the known date.[8] Already, in June 2005, Dalton McGuinty was seen to be preparing for 4 October (10, as it turned out) 2007.[9] Introducing the legislation in British Columbia on 21 August 2001 Attorney General Geoff Plant said, 'We now know when the next general election will be in British Columbia: May 17, 2005. Get ready now.'[10]

Fixed dates invite opposition foot dragging in the last months before an election. An opposition cannot hope to defeat government measures but it can hold them up for some time. Where governments have flexibility in choosing an election date, they can wait out opposition foot dragging. Because they can, it is less likely to occur.

Fixed terms necessarily prevent flexibility and convenience in election timing. The legislation in the provinces and Ottawa allows for small adjustments to take into account religious holidays or elections at other levels of government. There are many other legitimate factors – world and national events, leadership races, deaths of politicians, the legislative agenda, the weather and natural disasters – affecting when may be the best time for an election.

The theory that governments can receive a mandate for specific measures from an election victory is contested and obscure, but it is often widely felt that governments doing big new things should test their support in an election. Such things do not come up at a tidy quadrennial pace. As it happened, the Free Trade election of 1988 occurred at the conventional four-and-a-bit-years point after the election that brought the Mulroney government to power. With a fixed election date the election might have taken place either before the Free Trade Agreement, which was so much an issue, had been negotiated, or after it had been passed. The Liberal majority in the Senate had indicated that it would not pass the Free Trade Bill without an election. They could not have made such a stipulation with the election date fixed.

There is a risk that fixed terms will encourage the idea that prime ministers and premiers are entitled or obliged to serve their four years, regardless of what MPs or MLAs may think, feel, or do. In responsible parliamentary government, the prime minister or premier should serve only as long as he or she has enough support in the House to govern effectively. Based on misunderstandings, fixed-term legislation risks compounding misunderstandings. Stephen Harper insinuated in his 2006 year-end interview that he should be allowed to carry on until the proposed fixed date in October 2009.[11] As he prepared to call an election a year earlier, he complained that the opposition would not respect the fixed date.[12]

The subtly distracting effect of the fixed-term idea is at work. It is reasonable enough to talk of the Conservatives having won the 2006 election, but winning an election is not like winning a prize that you get to keep until the next tournament. The Conservatives were the most effective government available after the election. They had no claim to remain the government any longer than they remained the most effective government available. The parties represented in the House of Commons must make that judgment. They should not be distracted by any notion that the government should be allowed to 'serve out its term,' a 'term' that did not even exist at the time of the 2006 election, when there was only a limit to the life of Parliament and no one would have suggested that a minority government could or should serve to that limit.

Conversely Harper put himself in a fix by implying that he was obliged to live with the Thirty-ninth Parliament whatever it did, not free to advise a dissolution if he could not govern effectively. His one-time aide Tom Flanagan was moved to recommend brinksmanship,[13] acknowledging the unintended consequences of stupid legislation, which had inhibited Harper and emboldened the opposition and left observers wondering what Parliament could do. The opposition parties 'became noticeably more obstructionist' once the legislation had passed. Flanagan seems to have taken it for granted that Harper could not do what he did a year later and simply call an election when he felt the time was right.[14] Flanagan meant by brinksmanship that Harper should declare votes to be issues of confidence and dare the opposition to force an election. Harper seemed to be going to take his advice.[15] But, as I have explained, confidence is a matter of fact and not arbitrary stipulation. Had Harper waited for an electorally appealing issue of confidence we might have had months of ineffective government and game playing.

Sauce for the Gander

Stephen Harper's calling an election for 14 October 2008 and the protest that he had broken his own law, or at least the 'spirit' of that law, should have been an education in the folly of fixed election dates.

It is not only governments with a majority that have decided when elections will be held. When there is a minority government, the opposition parties can effectively decide when there will be an election, as happened in Ottawa in November 2005. This undoubtedly, and properly, was done on the calculation, which proved true, for some of them, that the opposition parties would better themselves in an election. No one blamed them for that. They could have been blamed, by their partisans, if they had voted down a government only to have it returned strengthened after an election, and by all of us, if there had been little change in party standings after the new election – though minority governments sometimes fall when no one has even a hunch what the election will bring, when simply no government can work with the House and all parties must take their chances with the voters.

Opposition parties under a minority government cannot just concern themselves with election timing. They do not directly decide when there will be an election. They have to let the government govern, at least tolerate a budget and some legislation, by abstaining or being conveniently absent, or the government will fall and there will be an election. Such principles as they have and their grass roots may impel them to defeat a government when the polls are against them. They may be wise to let the government govern even when they stand high in the polls, lest the voters turn against them.

If, with a minority government, the opposition can bring on an election, why should a minority government not be free to advise an election whenever it wants? The opposition could prevent an election by supporting another government, as the Dion coalition was ready to do. If they will not, they implicitly prefer an election to any government that could be formed from the opposition benches, and connive at the minority government's election call. Harper's election call never became a significant issue in the 2008 election because the opposition parties could not argue that they did not want an election. They only wanted one on a date of their choosing rather than Harper's.

Lester Pearson called an election in 1965 in the hope of winning a majority. He was disappointed. When a minority government decides on an election, its choice can, no more than with a majority government, be based on passing strength in the polls. A minority government calling an election judges that the voters have made up their minds enough to return a more effective government. It may be wrong. Pearson was in 1965. The Liberals had had a comfortable lead in the polls for more than a year. He did not reckon on Dief's continuing campaign strength, and, perhaps, public satisfaction with the existing Parliament, which had allowed the Liberals to govern effectively.

Opposition parties overturning a minority government should be as wary as majority governments of passing strength in the polls. Whatever the polls show from month to month, opposition parties must consider whether the minority government has been given a chance to show what it can do, whether the voters have really changed their preferences since the last election, or are simply expressing temporary irritation in opinion polls.

In practice, it is the majority of the House, whether in the form of a majority government or an opposition united against a minority government, that determines when, within the five-year life of Parliament, an election will be held. It cannot be fair that opposition parties should be able to gang up to force an election when they want, and unfair that a majority government should call an election when it wants. It would only be a problem if governments by choosing the perfect moment for an election could keep themselves in power indefinitely. But they cannot do that. The difference in practice is that with a minority gov-

ernment all parties can hope to improve their position. A majority government can only hope to hold its own.

To see election timing, whether on a government's call or on a united
opposition's defeat of a minority government, as simply attempts to
capitalize on strength in the polls abstracts from the substance of politics, issues, and records in office or opposition. It sees voters as reflected
in polls as creatures of mood, feeling, fashion, and whim. A government that turns to voters or an opposition that forces an election on that
basis risks its fate on what is inherently changeable. In a truer picture
a minority government courts defeat when it wants to do something
the opposition parties, because of what they are, will not stand, but the
voters will support, or the opposition unites to stop a minority government from doing what they think the voters do not want. The polls
may reflect the issues or they may be reflected in the polls only after the
election has been called.

Similarly a majority government cannot call an election to capture a
mood. It must run on its record, which, after years in office, is set, and
promises of more good things to come, which can be made to suit any
schedule and will only be credible if the record is creditable.

To reforming cynics, Harper did just what they wanted to prevent: he
called an election when he was strong in the polls, hoping for a majority. But he had been playing a game of chicken with the opposition for
almost three years. No one expected Parliament to last until the fixed
date. Dion, backed by his partners in waiting, was going to summon up
the courage to defeat the government at a date that was anything but
fixed. His repeated chickening out made it increasingly likely that he
would do so despite his persistent failure to gain strength in the polls.

The election call did not come out of nowhere. In February 2008
Harper was threatening to call an election if the Senate did not pass
an omnibus crime bill by 1 March, and it was generally accepted that,
whether or not he should, he could do so.[16]

Harper's meetings with the opposition leaders was seen as rather
a sham, but it would have taken only one to offer just a fraction of
the cooperation they promised each other three months later to derail
Harper's plan. More than for a majority, Harper's hope was simply
that, if he was returned with a strengthened minority, the continued
threat of defeat and an election would recede. He got what he wanted
and overplayed his new hand, leading to the extraordinary events of
December 2008. But there is simply no basis for saying that he got an
unfair advantage from not waiting for an election on 19 October 2009,

which would never have come. As it turned out, he probably could have got his majority in an election on that date.

Harper richly deserved what embarrassment, anxiety, and lowered esteem he may have suffered for calling the 14 October 2008 election. But his wrong was not in calling it but in introducing ill-considered legislation to pander to thoughtless Reform pieties and an uncomprehending public. It was partly a sham and partly irresponsibility. But the opposition parties who went along with it, with no more thought of being restricted by it, are in no position to criticize. We must do that for ourselves.

So far as the 'spirit' of the legislation is concerned, it is for the voters to judge. Their difficulty is that the call for fixed election dates has no 'spirit' behind it but a vague resentment of politicians and a desire to be left in peace. Appearing with officials before a Senate Committee in December 2006,[17] Justice Minister Rob Nicholson got into deep waters speculating what the governor general might do when faced with a request for a dissolution and an election contrary to what he described as the 'statutory expectation' created by the legislation. The legislation had been passed with unanimous smugness in the House of Commons but faced thoughtful and intelligent opposition from both Liberals and Conservatives in the Senate. Without quite saying so outright, Nicholson seemed to assume, as many did until well into 2008, that the legislation would prevent Harper from calling an election, though it would leave the opposition free to bring down the government and bring on an election. Everyone, including Stéphane Dion, assumed that there would be no breach of the legislation if the opposition precipitated an election.[18] It was assumed that the legislation 'effectively gave the Official Opposition the power to call the next election.'[19]

But simply by stating it, this understanding is revealed as preposterous. How could it be wrong for the government to precipitate an election and right for the opposition to do so? And, if sauce for the goose is sauce for the gander, why then should a majority government have less leeway than a minority government in choosing a date?

A Teachable Moment?

The reform lobby Democracy Watch launched a legal challenge to Harper's election call – an odd position for *soi-disant* champions of democracy to be objecting to an election, but let that be. It is plain on the face of the legislation that it was not breached, but as many have come to believe that anything they do not like must be against the law and the courts have been ready to hear them, if only to turn them away, reading the legislation is no help.

Democracy Watch allowed that there could be an early election after a non-confidence vote, conceding the right to precipitate an election to the opposition but not the government. After demolishing its arguments in detail, Mr Justice Michael Shore in the Federal Court excused Democracy Watch from the costs usually payable by losing litigants, on the basis that their challenge provided an opportunity to educate the public. It does not appear that the lesson is being learned, or this chapter would be shorter. Democracy Watch will not learn. After an appeal to the Federal Court of Appeal was briskly dismissed, it announced[20] that it would seek leave to appeal to the Supreme Court of Canada and claimed that the ruling meant that Harper broke an election promise to fix election dates and that it effectively cancelled the fixed legislation in seven provinces and the Northwest Territories.

Democracy Watch naturally has it in for Harper, but as the legislation is everywhere essentially the same and Harper was following provincial precedents, its argument is with all the politicians in government and opposition parties who practically unanimously and proudly supported the legislation whose meaning it refuses to understand.

In a Pickle

The attempts to fix election dates by statute revealed the folly of the idea and the difficulties it must lead to. Under parliamentary government, an election date can never really be fixed in advance because it is, or should, always be possible that the government will be defeated. Because the provinces are barred from changing their constitutions in any way affecting the powers of the lieutenant governors, the provincial acts affirm that the lieutenant governor may dissolve the legislative assembly when he or she sees fit. As the lieutenant governor would generally act on the advice of the government, it can be, and was, argued that the legislation is effete.[21] For similar reasons,[22] the Ottawa legislation affirms the governor general's power to dissolve Parliament 'at [her] discretion.'

If there were no constitutional restrictions, fixed-date election legislation would have to try to codify what cannot be codified, to set out rules for determining when there should be an election outside the four-year schedule. Whether a government is capable of governing with an existing House is a matter of judgment – a judgment the governor general, or a lieutenant governor, must make. It is usually simple enough. No one could have supposed that Joe Clark's government could have continued after its budget defeat in December 1979. But where a government does not have assured command of the House, it might be defeated on some measures without its ability to govern being necessarily at an end. Generally reformers are keen that this should be possible. Or a government might accept repeated defeats on important matters, losing the power to govern, but clinging to office and refusing to call an election. In such circumstances it could be the duty of the governor to call an election without the advice of the government. The governor's responsibility is to see that there is a government – a government in fact, not just in name, supported, or at least tolerated, by a majority of the Commons or the legislative assembly. If no government can be effective in a particular Commons or assembly, there must be a dissolution, whatever the government in name may wish.

Nor can it be passed on to the Commons or the legislative assembly to decide when an election should be called. A private member's bill that preceded the Ontario legislation obscurely attempted to do that. It said an election could be called 'where a majority of members of the Legislative Assembly, including a majority of the members who do not belong to the party from which the Government is chosen, have demonstrated a lack of confidence in the Government.'[23] It is perfectly possible that a House could regularly defeat the government on important measures but refuse to vote for a motion of non-confidence, withdrawing its confidence in practice but refusing to admit it by express resolution. Everything from a mere desire to secure a pension, to fear of personal electoral defeat, to a bloody-minded desire to see a government stew in impotence for a while could keep a Parliament going when it could no longer be the basis for effective government, if the choice of an election date was left to the House itself. It is no evident advance that the life of Parliament should be up to its members, or, as the private member's bill seemed to contemplate, to the opposition members. No statute can set out rules for all possibilities.

Everyone knew when the opposition in Ottawa united to vote for a non-confidence motion on 28 November 2005 that an election must follow, and in that sense the opposition decided that there should be an election. But they were not voting on when the election should be. They had done that a few days before, calling for an election on 13 February 2006, but the vote had no legal force and the government, quite rightly, ignored it. The opposition was trying to avoid blame for an election campaign over Christmas. In the end, no one seemed to mind it. But it would be wrong to leave a government in office that had lost the confidence of the House, and that was what the opposition was trying to do.

Some European countries, not having had the good fortune, which reformers are so keen to cast aside, to receive their political institutions from a long-evolved tradition, have tried in their constitutions to codify the supple pragmatism of parliamentary government. Pragmatism finds ways of getting round the rules. When German Chancellor Gerhard Schroeder decided in the summer of 2005 that he wanted an election called a year before the fixed date, even though he had a majority, he arranged a no-confidence vote in which members of his own party abstained to precipitate an election. It had been done before, by Helmut Kohl in 1983.

The even handed-official Legislative Summary[24] published with the Harper government's bill lists as arguments for it:

- It would remove an element of unpredictability from Canada's political system, and provide a degree of security of tenure for the House of Commons and the government …
- It would give governments reasonable and sufficient time to develop and implement their legislative agenda or program, without the risk of having to fight an election, and it would allow some of the more difficult and unpopular decisions to be taken.
- It would remove the threat of dissolution, which is a major factor used by governing parties to keep their members and supporters in line; it could, therefore, lead to more independence for ordinary Members of Parliament, and more relaxed party discipline …
- Opposition parties, knowing that the government has a fixed term of office, might be more constructive in their criticism, and develop different approaches.

As the legislation expressly protects the power of dissolution, and its promoters argue that it will make no difference to the responsibility of governments to the Commons and the possibility of defeat, followed by an election, these arguments express only confusion. Behind the confusion may lurk a wish for real fixed terms, such as there are in the United States, either in some who prefer the United States Constitution but are afraid to admit it, or in some who are too stupid to know what real fixed terms would mean.

If there is a minority government, there cannot be, ought not to be, 'security of tenure for the House of Commons and the government' or 'reasonable and sufficient time to develop and implement their legislative agenda or program.' With a minority government, dissolution is not a threat but a real risk, which the government party must daily face. Opposition parties facing a minority government are, by their lights quite rightly, not interested in being constructive but in replacing the government.

Majority governments already have more than 'a degree of security of tenure.' They have five years 'to develop and implement their legislative agenda or program.' The threat of dissolution under a majority government is no more than a reminder to its members that they are a team, which, if it does not play as a team, will be defeated. The threat is as much in the hands of the members as of the government. A dissolution and election brought on by a rebellion of government MPs would likely lead to defeat at the polls.

The fixed-date legislation provides, in the event of an election out of schedule, that the next election will be on whichever is the chosen date, in May or October, in the fourth calendar year after that election. The intent is evident to fix the schedule and the 'term' in any event. Depending on when the out-of-schedule election fell, the time between elections could be as little as forty-six months or as much as fifty-seven months. The original 19 October 2009 date fixed in the Harper legislation did not follow its own formula in providing for an election only forty-five months after the previous election held in 23 January 2006.

The next election is now supposed to be on 15 October 2012. No one expects the Fortieth Parliament to last that long, but there is no reason why Ignatieff, Layton, and Duceppe should decide when it will end rather than Harper.

While providing for elections roughly every four years, the Harper bill does not purport to shorten the five-year life of Parliament provided for under the Constitution Act. It would require a constitutional amendment to change that. If the governor general's discretion is truly unaffected by the bill, he or she is not obliged to dissolve Parliament for an election scheduled for whatever is the next fixed date. Presumably the prime minister would advise a dissolution in time for the election, and the governor general would follow the advice. But the theoretical possibility that she or he might not, illustrates the confusion of drafters trying to turn a Parliament with a limit to its life into a Parliament with a fixed term.

Fixed election dates is a reform by which all reasonable considerations in election timing are excluded so that the thing that never could happen can be prevented. To the extent that it changes anything, a reform promoted by politicians ostensibly to limit their power and promote public trust must end by giving them more job security and making them less effective and responsible. The legislation should be repealed. If politicians with a crack at forming a government want to promise not to go to the polls for four years, they may do so, and live with the consequences.

3 Out of Proportion:
Proportional Representation

The reform most widely and loudly demanded, which would have the most devastating impact on government, is electoral reform, changing the rules by which those who represent us, and decide who will govern us, are chosen. This is most often advanced as a claim for proportional representation, matching a party's share of seats in the House of Commons to its share of the popular vote.

Advocates of proportional representation are fond of figures: in the general election of 2004 New Democrat candidates got 15.7 per cent of the vote but only 6.1 per cent of the seats in the House of Commons; in the general election of 2000 Liberal candidates got 40.8 per cent of the vote but 57.1 per cent of the seats; in the New Brunswick election of 1987 Progressive Conservative candidates got 28.6 per cent of the vote but no seats. People who have not thought about proportional representation may think these figures mean something. But they mean nothing unless you have already decided that parties should get seats in proportion to the votes their candidates get. Why should they? Proponents of proportional representation claim many fancied benefits from it. Its opponents have strong pragmatic reasons for their rejection of it. But proportional representation is a dogmatic error rather than a pragmatic misjudgment.

The dogma that parties should have seats in proportion to the votes they get is not argued for but assumed. The insistent claim of advocates of proportional representation that it is fairer simply begs the question, what is fairer about it? Each party gets its fair share of seats? But is politics for parties? Is it not about government? Can government be broken up and handed out like cake? Elections are not about sharing. They are about the people deciding.

They say that proportional representation is more democratic because it makes every vote count when, without it, the votes of those who vote for a losing candidate (or whose votes are more than a winning candidate needs) are, they say, wasted. Counts for what? The argument is circular. Of course under proportional representation every vote counts towards the seats the parties get, because that is what the proportional representation does: it gives seats to parties in proportion to the votes they get. The question why it should do that remains unanswered. The only evident answer is that it is done because it can be done.

If proportionality and making every citizen's vote count is the goal, why should we apply it to parties and not to policies? If 50 per cent of the people oppose capital punishment and 40 per cent support it and 10 per cent are undecided, why should we not give five out of ten murderers a life sentence, hang four, and keep one on death row until the undecided make up their minds? To govern is to choose. In a democracy there are always winners and losers, whatever the electoral system and even when direct democracy through referendums is practised. No electoral system can get around that fact, and what results from it: that most people, most of the time, will be unhappy with much of what governments do. The only way to limit that is to limit government, but that is another subject.

Government is not a jumble of discreet choices, of which some people could make some, and others, with different ideas and interests, could make others. The choices must fit together. This is most obvious in a budget. We cannot cut taxes, raise spending, and reduce debt. But we cannot have a right-wing foreign policy and a left-wing defence policy. Proportional government is impossible. However, as we shall see, proportional representation can give parties disproportionate shares in government and power.

In elections where the position at stake is not a seat in a legislature but an executive position, as with the mayors in most Canadian cities, the issue of proportional representation and wasted votes is not raised. David Miller was elected mayor of Toronto in 2003 with 43.58 per cent of the votes against 38.33 per cent for John Tory, 9.23 per cent for Barbara Hall, 5.24 per cent for John Nunziata, and 0.71 per cent for Tom Jakobek. Should each of the losers have got to be mayor for a number of days, or hours, proportionate to the votes they got? Were the votes for the losers wasted if they did not?

Why Parties?

It is parties that advocates of proportional representation think should be the beneficiaries of proportionality. Why? What are parties for?

There are all kinds of associations that promote the interests and ideas that are the stuff of politics. Historically many did, and some still do, support candidates in elections. During elections, candidates are faced with scores of requests from groups asking them where they stand on their issues. The responses are published with either explicit or implicit endorsements of the candidates who answer correctly. But, to be a party as generally understood, an association must put up candidates selected by its own rules and run some kind of campaign on behalf of them. Any association that does that assumes a responsibility for all that governments may do, even if the legalization of marijuana or the independence of Quebec or farmers' interests are what got them into politics, and even if their position on everything else is indifference or that nothing should be done. That is a position in itself, and the one-issue or one-interest party will have to contend not only with those who oppose the legalization of marijuana or whatever but with those who insist that other issues have to be addressed and other interests weighed. MPs are called to deal with all our public business. They cannot choose to deal with only some of it. Nor can voters, in choosing an MP, limit themselves to some issues and interests. Government will not.

Parliament had a long history before there were parties. MPs in a Tudor House of Commons may have seen things differently, depending on whether they represented London, or a borough, or a county seat. But there were no parties. Even when the divisions between Cavaliers and Roundheads or Tories and Whigs emerged in the seventeenth century there were no organizations and no labels beyond insults hurled across the political divides. Men ran as individuals, and at an election the voters might have to choose between two Whigs or two Tories and someone who did not know what he was.

It was only with the coming of what is now known as responsible government in the early eighteenth century that parties finally emerged. As responsibility for government came to be assumed by a ministry drawn from Parliament and supported by the House of Commons, it became necessary to organize that support and seek its continuance in elections. Nothing at all like modern party organization emerged until well into the nineteenth century. But in Parliament, and at elections, parties finally emerged as the purpose for which they exist emerged.

A party exists to form a government. It is a political association of people whose interests and ideas and confidence in each other make it possible that they should be able to work together to support coherent measures, a ministry, and, most important, a budget. No party has any value in politics unless it is a potential government. Any political association can call itself a party. If it promotes only one issue or interest, or if it so positions itself that it can never hope to form a government, it cannot serve the purpose for which parties exist and does not deserve the name.

A so-called party that has no hope of forming a government is necessarily a fraud and undemocratic. It cannot honestly promise to do anything because it will never, by itself, be able to do anything. It offers what it cannot deliver. Its goals can only be achieved with the help of others who share its goals and are therefore equally worthy of the votes of its supporters, or others who are prepared to support something they do not believe in for the sake of power, making a corrupt bargain and allowing a minority to lever a balance of power in a fragmented Parliament – fragmented most likely by proportional representation – to get what it wants against the will of the majority.

Once parties are understood in light of the purpose for which they exist, the absurdity of giving them seats in proportion to their candidates' votes is evident. Parties cannot be given a share of government in proportion to their votes. A government so constituted would be incoherent and paralytic. Giving seats in Parliament in proportion to votes for parties can be done, but it makes no sense. It proportions two means to a party's end of forming a government – votes and seats – and in so doing subverts the end. No party can any longer hope to form a government. Proportional representation's assurance of seats to parties that can neither hope nor intend to form a government by themselves means that elections do not decide who governs. A coalition becomes necessary to form a government. What the coalition may be cannot be known until after the election. The voters can have no say on it. Parties haggle in secret over shares in a government that was not on offer in the election and could not be foreseen.

Responsible government led naturally to the growth of two parties: the party of those supporting the government and the party of those opposing it and hoping to replace it, the party of an alternative government. People of all opinions and interests found a place in one party or the other where they could work together in support of a government. Each party sought to encompass whatever opinions and interests it could work with to bolster its strength.

Once the House of Commons in effect decided who would be the government, the most important thing about a candidate seeking to be a member became, for most voters, whom he would support in government. By choosing a Whig or a Tory, the voter could effectively have a say in who would govern. For some voters, the character and standing of the candidate was still more important than his party. By making the candidate only a counter for a party, a party incapable of governing by itself, proportional representation makes party affiliation the legal determinant of who gets elected, but the reason why it should matter – its effect on who governs – is gone, as the party can never govern.

If voters generally will not give majority support to one party when several are on offer, why should our elections produce majority governments, as generally they do? Because elections are a means for letting the voters decide. Under proportional representation voters are allowed, even forced, to cast votes that do not produce a decision. Every interest or tendency in the electorate is photographically reproduced, but who will govern and how is decided after the election. Proportional representation's supporters' abstraction from the real work of politics – and the purpose of parties and pursuit of an arithmetic relation between votes and parties – relieves or bars voters from deciding.

Political scientists sometimes write as if our way of voting were devised to produce majority governments. Some suggest a skewed proportional representation that would give bigger parties a disproportionate share of seats in order to try to produce majority governments while keeping some degree of proportional representation – a kind of proportional representation for the opposition. But our way of voting was not devised for majority governments, or parties or government at all. It was devised to produce representatives from across England who could vote money for the King and pass laws as they were needed. The King governed.

When, after the conflicts of the seventeenth century, it was settled that the government should have the support of the House of Commons, a government majority formed naturally and practically (fuelled by liberal patronage). It was not the application of a political theory. Common ground and mutual confidence sufficient to govern was found as it was needed. Elections were not designed to produce majorities. Majorities were needed for government once it became responsible to the House of Commons and parties formed to produce them and sustain them. There was, and is, no point in accommodating and sustaining factions incapable of governing. It needed no theory to see that. It was a practical matter, as government is a practical matter. Proportional representation invites and encourages politicians to form hypothetical governments, theoretical governments. What they will do in practice they cannot say. They work that out after the elections.

PR for Parties, Parties for PR

Proportional representation's supporters argue as if the way we elect members now, what they sneeringly call the 'First Past the Post System,' were a terrible mistake, an archaic invention, that modern ingenuity should leave behind. It is condemned because it does not yield proportional representation of parties, as if the purpose of Parliament was to serve the parties. But it is the other way around. Parties were formed to allow Parliament to work and to support a government. Parliament does not exist to allow parties to fragment government and haggle over it.

With proportional representation every interest, faction, tendency, ideology, ethnic or regional bloc, or theory has an incentive to break off and form its own party. The politicians, who are popularly supposed to oppose electoral reform for selfish reasons, are relieved of the responsibility to work together and are set free to run their own shows, taking their chances in bargaining for power in coalitions, but assured of seats for the party insiders.

In Europe, where proportional representation is common, by the time effective parliamentary government came there generally already existed several political movements unwilling to accept anything that would have impelled them to coalesce into potential governing parties. Proportional representation is the political drug of choice for small parties. It has only become an issue where there are third or fourth parties, which, whatever their original ambitions, have evidently no hope of winning a majority of seats. We did not hear much of proportional representation from the Co-operative Commonwealth Federation (CCF) or the New Democratic Party (NDP) when, buoyed by provincial victories, their faith was that they could one day form a government in Ottawa. Despairing of breaking out of the teens in the popular vote, Jack Layton now demands proportional representation.

The Green Party, not wanting to bother trying to appeal to most voters, wants to get into Parliament with 5 per cent of the vote. Projecting idealism untainted by power, perfectly irresponsible, new parties like the Greens attract sympathy in their call for proportional representation.

Proportional representation takes time to do its work. After the Greens it might be years before another party emerged from a new political movement or a party split. But once it did emerge, proportional representation would see that it stayed. Proportional representation will keep small parties going indefinitely. They have no incentive to merge or seek broader support.

What? A Waste?

Because it makes no sense, proportional representation cannot solve the imaginary problem of wasted votes that it is supposed to address and leads to many real problems. It does not assure that no votes are wasted or every vote counts in deciding who will govern: that every voter gets a say in government. Notoriously, the Communist Party of Italy, under perhaps the most famous example of proportional representation in practice, consistently got around 20 to 30 per cent of the vote in elections, but for over forty years the Communists never formed part of the government or even exercised leverage on who did form the government. Governments were formed and fell and elections were held, and none of the tens of millions of votes cast for the Communists had any direct effect. The votes cast for the Communists were as much wasted as are, under the theory of proportional representation, votes for losing candidates.

Proportional representation's advocates say that votes for losing candidates and excess votes for winning candidates are wasted. But if the measure of whether a vote is wasted is its impact on government, votes for parties that win seats but never enter government or for parties that are always in government, whatever the fluctuations of their votes, are as much wasted.

And votes for losing candidates or excess votes for winning candidates are not wasted. They are markers for the future. Those for losing candidates show a base from which future winners may come. Excess votes for winning candidates show strength to spare should unpopular decisions be necessary.

In the theory of proportional representation most votes in our elections and elections in many other countries are wasted as not being necessary for the election of a winning candidate. Most of those votes are cast by voters who know that their candidate is either sure to win or sure to lose, but in the face of all the carping voters in their billions cast their votes anyway. They see the point when the proponents of proportional representation refuse to. Those proponents could not come up with the figures they are so fond of, showing what they claim are wasted votes, if voters were not so keen to, as they see it, waste their votes.

The notion of the wasted vote is an artefact of proportional representation dogma. You could say you wasted your vote if you did not vote, as, if you had a ticket to a ball game and did not go, you would say you wasted your ticket. Or you could say you wasted your vote if you spoilt your ballot. But to say you have wasted your vote if your vote does not count, in however miniscule a degree, towards a party winning a seat, amounts to saying that your vote is wasted if it does not produce a winner. With proportional representation in Canada every vote would count for 0.00002 seats. But the price of this tiny victory would be loss of control over who governs. It is only when you accept the proportional representation argument that every vote must count towards seats that the phrase *wasted vote* takes on meaning. When you vote for Jones for mayor, and Singh wins or Jones wins by a landslide, you do not think you wasted your vote.

Voting is a procedure for letting the people decide. If they are not unanimous, any decision must involve one choice winning and another losing. The proportional representation goal that 'everyone wins and all get prizes' means the voters do not decide. That is a real waste of voting.

Imbalance of Power

Proportional representation's most notorious and perverse effect is a disproportionate influence for small parties. The transparent ambition of the New Democrats is to hold the balance of power in a Parliament in which no party can ever win a majority. The Green Party seeks to be its rival in holding the balance of power.

With the balance of power comes disproportionate power. A party for which only a few issues matter, like the small religious parties in Israel, can impose its will on those issues against the majority of voters by giving its support to whichever coalition is prepared to buy its votes by satisfying its demands. Parties with a less specific agenda can bargain for a more or less permanent disproportionate share in government. The German Free Democrats started out as a free market liberal party, arguably to the right of the Christian Democrats. In time they came to be a centrist party shifting their support to the Social Democrats so long as their oversized share in the government was guaranteed. Between 1949 and 1998 they were in the government for forty-one years, always providing the deputy chancellor and holding a larger share of the Cabinet than even their share of seats in the majority coalition indicated. With only about 6 per cent of the vote, they decided who would govern, backing the second-place Social Democrats in 1969 and shifting to the Christian Democrats in 1982, each time without an election.

Germany's *Sonderweg*

Germany's system of proportional representation seemed for forty years to yield stable and responsible government. It was held up as an ideal and happy medium, with a 5 per cent threshold to keep out fringe parties and half the members of the Bundestag elected in constituencies. In fact Germany's proportional representation is real proportional representation, the 5 per cent threshold only a small protection against its dangers and the constituency elections strictly subordinate to proportional representation. The German election of 2005 showed that it does not work.

The peculiar circumstances of post-war West Germany meant that the range of parties common in the rest of Europe did not exist and could not easily be started up. There resulted a kind of two-and-a-half-party system. The role of the Free Democrats was seen as a benign moderating influence on whichever of the big parties, Christian Democrat or Social Democrat, it chose to support, though if either the Christian Democrats or the Social Democrats needed moderating, it was only because, under proportional representation, the narrow middle of the road was occupied by the Free Democrats. The role of the Free Democrats was an accident of German politics. In time the party weakened as it came to stand for nothing but holding onto a too large share of power. Its survival depended to some extent on the tactical votes of supporters of whichever major party expected it to be its coalition partner. Only a small shift of votes in 1969 would have brought the far right National Democrats into the Bundestag.

After the election of 2005 neither a Free Democrat / Christian Democrat nor a Green / Social Democrat coalition could achieve a majority. The Christian Democrats would have needed to include the Greens, to the left of the Social Democrats, as well as the Free Democrats, to achieve a majority. The Social Democrats, even with the Greens, would have had to depend on the Left Party, a mix of ex-Communists and renegade Social Democrats, to achieve a majority, giving that dodgy group with 8.7 per cent of the vote a life-and-death hold on the government.

A grand coalition between the Christian Democrats and Social Democrats, who together won almost 70 per cent of the votes, was formed under the Christian Democrat leader Angela Merkel. Polls showed that such a coalition was the third choice of voters with only 25 per cent support, behind a Social Democrat / Free Democrat / Green coalition favoured by 27 per cent and a Christian Democrat / Free Democrat / Green coalition favoured by 33 per cent.[25] But under proportional representation the voters do not choose the government and what they told pollsters was meaningless.

Advocates of proportional representation brush aside arguments that the 2005 election showed the faults in what had appeared to be the most successful proportional representation regime. They say that the Grand Coalition had the support of 70 per cent of the voters. But no one voted for a Grand Coalition. Presumably those who voted Christian Democrat wanted a Christian Democrat government and those who voted Social Democrat wanted a Social Democrat government.

After the election some Christian Democrat and some Social Democrat voters may have felt that half a government was better than none. But some may not. Many must have voted Social Democrat precisely to keep the Christian Democrats out of power or Christian Democrat to get rid of the Social Democrats. One is tempted to say that their votes were wasted.

The only important change in the voting between the previous election in 2002 and the election in 2005 was a surge in support for the Left Party, which went from 4.0 per cent to 8.7 per cent in the popular vote and won fifty-four seats. But under proportional representation a surge in support for a left-wing party produced in the Grand Coalition a government to the right of the one before the election.

The election had been a hard-fought contest between the Christian Democrats and the Social Democrats, each saying what fine things they would do and why the other's plans and people would be bad for Germany. Two months later they were colleagues, wrapped in a 60,000 word Coalition Agreement that premises discipline in both parties that would make Jean Chrétien's rule look anarchic, with all actions to be thrashed out in joint party committees. Polls showed that 74 per cent of Germans thought that politicians negotiating the Coalition Agreement were concerned about their careers and personal development against only 20 per cent who thought they were concerned with actual political issues.[26]

It says little for the probity of German politics that an election that was all about why one party rather than the other should govern produced an agreement that both should. The election showed that, while in our elections the voters effectively decide who governs, proportional representation takes the decision out of their hands.

If asking voters in a poll what coalition they preferred was meaningless, asking them to vote for a party is also meaningless. What, one wonders, did the 9.8 per cent of German voters who voted Green want? Did they actually want a Green government? The Green Party knew it could not form a government and so did the voters. Or did they want a government 9.8 per cent Green? They did not get it. To that end many would have done better to vote Social Democrat, because there would be no Greens in government unless the Social Democrats remained strong.

Angela Merkel briefly had a high personal approval rating in the polls, but soon she and her government were rated unsatisfactory by most in polls, and both parties in the coalition saw their support drop sharply while the parties excluded saw theirs rise. The Grand Coalition had difficulty making decisions but there was no effective opposition.

After the last Grand Coalition, in the election of 1969, the Christian Democrats were comfortably ahead of the Social Democrats with 46 per cent of the vote against 42 per cent for the Social Democrats. But the Free Democrats, resentful at being left out of government for three years, and fearful of Christian Democrat talk of doing away with proportional representation, chose that moment to throw their 6 per cent around and went into a coalition with the Social Democrats.

In the election of 2009 Merkel ran what was called a 'Valium campaign.'[27] The Christian Democrats and their rivals were still serving in government together. Merkel could not run on a record shared with the Social Democrats without implicitly endorsing them. She allowed that she hoped for a coalition with the Free Democrats but she could not count on it and would not campaign vigorously against the Social Democrats with whom she might have to continue in coalition.

The only excitement in the campaign was attacks by the Social Democrats on the Free Democrats as rivals for a coalition under Merkel and the Christian Democrats, and Free Democrats on the prospect of a Social Democrat coalition with the Left Party, forsworn by the Social Democrats despite their willingness to enter coalitions with the Left Party at the state level.

The German edition of the *Financial Times* endorsed Merkel but quixotically hoped for a Christian Democrat coalition with the Greens and to that end urged voters *not* to vote Green lest they should be strong enough to form a coalition with the Social Democrats.[28]

The English edition of the *Financial Times* pronounced the German voting system broken.[29]

Over 4 million fewer votes were cast in 2009 than in 2005, and in the result both coalition parties lost votes, the Social Democrats gaining the lowest share of the vote in their history, while all the parties excluded from the coalition gained votes, the Free Democrats, out of power for eleven years, making their best showing ever. Germany appeared to have returned to form with a Christian Democrat / Free Democrat coalition much like those that have ruled for most of the history of the Federal Republic. A marked increase in the right-wing parties' share of the vote produced a more right-wing government. It was neither divine intervention nor a fluke. A strong enough trend in voting will produce a result, even with proportional representation. But with five parties now contending for a share in government at both the federal and state levels, there will be fluke results and a need for divine intervention in the years to come.

Throw the Bums Out

In the first forty-nine years of the German Federal Republic no government was defeated in an election. Only the decisions of the Free Democrats brought down governments, without regard to any preferences shown by the voters.

It is the ability to 'throw the bums out,' more even than the ability to choose a new government, that is the most striking practical virtue of our present way of voting. Our governments are responsible, must answer to the voters, and are regularly defeated. Joseph Schumpeter[30] and Karl Popper[31] saw the ability to get rid of an unsatisfactory government as the purpose and test of democracy and condemned proportional representation for not seeing this. To 'throw the bums out' is almost impossible with proportional representation. In the fifty years after 1945 in 103 elections in Belgium, Germany, Italy, Japan, the Netherlands, Sweden, and Switzerland, the major governing party was thrown from office only six times.[32] Major parties have remained in government for decades under proportional representation despite wide fluctuations in their votes. Minor parties often seem to share in government in inverse proportion to their electoral success, turfed out when their vote grows and they look threatening and brought in when it sags.

Looking at shares in government over the long term, Liberals and Conservatives in Canada and Labour and Conservatives in Britain have approached a rough proportion to their votes. Under German proportional representation, on the other hand, the Free Democrats in five decades had almost the same share of time in Cabinet seats as the Social Democrats, who had won four times as many votes.

It can hardly be said that German proportional representation produced the government the voters wanted. In Canada, by contrast, after the election of 23 January 2006, in which Conservatives got 36 per cent of the votes, polls showed 36 per cent wanted the minority government to last four years, 22 per cent two years, and 23 per cent one.[33] In the week after Stephen Harper's government was sworn in, 54 per cent approved of it.[34] Ten days later, 46 per cent thought the Conservatives would be a better government than the Liberals had been and 32 per cent the same.[35]

Bad Tactics, Uncertain Coalitions

There is much talk in our elections of tactical voting – voting not for the best candidate or your favourite party but for the candidate most likely to defeat the candidate of the party you hate. The proportional representation enthusiast sees tactical voting as an attempt to avoid wasting a vote under a faulty electoral system. Under proportional representation, they argue, voting is simple. You just vote for your favourite party with the assurance that your vote will be reflected in the number of seats it will get. But, if the relation between votes and seats is made simple, all too simple, the relation between votes and government is not. You may choose to vote for party F and be part of a surge of support for that party, which, on the theory of proportionality, should give it more strength in government. But if parties necessary for a coalition government with party F weaken, perhaps partly because of party F's strength, party F may end up with more seats but less strength, even out of government altogether.

Under proportional representation the voter has to consider not just his choice of party but the likely strength of that party's possible coalition partners and what coalitions might be formed without the chosen party. Usually it is not just difficult but impossible to foresee these things. If parties went into elections as coalitions, this difficulty would be reduced, but that would effectively result in a two-party system, which it is practically the intention of proportional representation to avoid. Parties under proportional representation may say what they would do in government if they could, but they cannot be held responsible for what they say during elections because elections do not decide who will govern. Post-election coalition bargaining decides who will govern, and on election day the voter can have only the vaguest grasp of how the bargaining may go and how to influence it in voting.

Under proportional representation, coalition governments are the norm, but, come the election, the parties go their separate ways. If two or more parties can work effectively together in government, they should merge. To work together effectively in government is the point of parties. Proportional representation is blind to that. It encourages parties to remain separate, even to split. The parties to a coalition may wish to choose new partners for their next dance in government.

The best measure of how people will govern is their record in government. Manifestos, proclaimed principles, and policies mean little until put to the test of choosing in government and facing its day-to-day challenges, beyond anticipation in an election. Our governments are often said to run on their record and, conversely, it is a commonplace, in our politics, that governments defeat themselves, unable to satisfy the voters who may be rightly sceptical of the claims of the opposition, preferring the devil they know in government, until arrogance, incompetence, or corruption persuades them to take a chance on change. With coalition governments and multi-party elections no one owns the record. The government the voters have known is not running. If it gave satisfaction, there is no guarantee its components will coalesce after the election. However bad it was, much of it will likely be back after the election.

Where proportional representation does its work and sustains a large number of parties, coalitions can be unstable, and governments will change often between elections without voters having any say. The instability of governments is a problem in itself, but what makes it worse is that it can be accompanied by stagnation. Italy had forty-seven governments between 1945 and 1995 but the Christian Democrats dominated them all.

The full range of parties encouraged by proportional representation's emphasis on parties and blindness to the purpose for which parties exist, best exemplified in Italy in the heyday of proportional representation, shows the absurd results of an absurd system. The parties were not a simple line-up of fine gradations along the crude left/right political spectrum with regional or sectional variations. The Christian

Democratic Party was a broad tent, some of whose members might just as well have been moderate Communists, while at the other extreme its members stopped just short of neo-fascism. The Liberals, the Republicans, the Social Democrats, and the Socialists could all have found a comfortable home with the Christian Democrats, but personal rivalries, institutional histories, and the encouragement of proportional representation sustained them.

In Canada we expect, if no party gets a majority, that there will be another election in about two years. In Italy and other countries with proportional representation, the instability of governments does not generally lead to frequent elections. Governments might fall four or more times between elections and each time a new government would be formed without the voters having any say. When they are held, elections do little or nothing to ease the formation of a stable government. Voting shifts from election to election are not great and consequently, under proportional representation, the composition of parliaments does not change much. Voters can neither reward nor punish parties that may have been in and out of government since the last election and can plead that it is some other party's fault if they did not do wonderful things. However much voters may want to get rid of a government, or establish it on a firm footing, there is little they can do to that end, and voters tend to troop out from one election to another and vote for their team. In Canada, an election can produce a change in government or end a parliamentary stalemate. In countries with proportional representation, elections change little.

Token MPs

As proportional representation sees votes as votes for parties rather than individuals, it has drastic implications for MPs. One theme of the democratic reform lobby is that MPs should be able to vote freely. For MPs this means free to vote as they wish, and for some voters free to vote as the voters instruct. But the logic of proportional representation reduces MPs to mere party tokens. Party X gets 17 per cent of the vote and should be entitled to 53 tokens in the parliamentary game. In practice, even politicians have enough character to resist becoming mere tokens, and their room for manoeuvre varies in the various countries with proportional representation. But the logic of proportional representation, under which MPs only get into Parliament because they are on the party list, implies that they should always act strictly as a party tool. If they are allowed to stray, what proportional representation understands as the will of the voters will be frustrated. Instead of getting the 17 per cent of party X in Parliament their votes in theory entitle them to they get 0.3 per cent Cohen, and 0.3 per cent Lee, and so on.

Carried to its logical conclusion, proportional representation should do away with MPs altogether. Each party should simply get voting points in proportion to the votes cast for it, which could be carried to any number of decimal points. The party, in accordance with its own internal rules, by politburo decision or after grass roots consultation, could deploy its points as it saw fit, provide ministers, if it formed part of a governing coalition, drawn from any walk of life, and have local offices across the country to provide the services MPs try to provide through their constituency offices. Opposition parties could operate as think tanks.

Proportional representation elections usually work by party lists. Each party offers an ordered list of candidates, and in the case of party X the top 53 on the list are elected. The voters could be supposed to be voting, not for a party, but for the nice bunch of people on the X list. In some countries voters can indicate their own preference among the candidates on the party list. But in practice, in any proportional representation election the party machine decides who will sit in the legislature, depending on how many votes the party gets. As is implied by the principles of proportional representation, the individual member is the tool of the party. The internal workings of parties, which, however broad their membership, always involve obscurely only a small minority of voters, become dangerously important.

In most proportional representation systems there are no by-elections, and vacancies are filled by names lower down the list. All attempts to give voters a say beyond what the party lists decree, if they have any effect, simply confuse the dogmatic simplicity of proportional representation, which is sold as a way of allowing the legislature to reflect precisely the party preferences of voters.

For some advocates of proportional representation, the parties' control of who gets elected is appealing for a paradoxical reason. They want more women or members of ethnic groups elected, and parties in preparing lists can engage in a little affirmative action. For these high-minded types, part of the appeal of proportional representation is that, under the guise of making every vote count, it gives party elites a chance to choose the people who ought to be elected, when voters left to their own choices fail to do so.

Proportional representation necessarily breaks the connection between the voter and the member. Whether we voted for the winner or not, we all have our member of Parliament. We know that and, perhaps more important, the member knows that and will be solicitous of the voters to a fault. Our MP represents everyone in the riding, hoping to win over those who voted for someone else and fearing the loss of supporters from the last election. The MP under proportional representation represents only the party voters. Other parties' MPs must represent other parties' voters. Appealing to the voters generally is not important. Even keeping the party's voters happy is secondary to the MP whose future depends more on ranking on the party list decided by the party apparatus, than on popularity with the party's voters.

Whether proportional representation's members are from one national list or several regional lists, the link with local voters is broken. Germany pretends to have the best of both worlds with half (roughly; it gets very complicated) the members elected in one-member ridings. A party with less than 5 per cent of the vote can elect a member if one of its candidates wins in a riding. But proportional representation is strictly enforced, and a candidate who trailed in a riding poll may be elected if the party is entitled to enough seats. Most members of the Bundestag do not represent a riding. Germany's attempt to retain a vestige of local representation is another admission that proportional representation's dogma entails ignoring what elections are for.

Going Soft

Several countries attempt to meet the objection that proportional representation leads to a proliferation of parties by stipulating a threshold of votes below which a party gets no seats. Germany's 5 per cent rule is the best-known example. This kind of rule, the possibility of voters expressing their preferences within a party list, and the fact that members of legislatures chosen by proportional representation are still generally free to jump from their party – though they rarely do – are presented by advocates of proportional representation as answers to its critics. The implication is that the critics caricature proportional representation and its advocates show proportional representation with a human face, its edges softened.

But proportional representation rests on a dogma. If parties should get seats in proportion to votes cast, then in any legislature with more than fifty seats, getting 2 per cent of the vote should mean getting at least one seat. If members get their seats only because of votes for the party, they should be expected to follow the straight party line. Any departure from the logic of proportional representation's dogma becomes a pragmatic calculation dependent on a likely temporary political conjuncture.

Some people advocate what the Law Commission of Canada calls 'an element of proportionality.'[36] They see the practical problems with proportional representation but not the theoretical error. They want to be nice to proportional representation's unyielding proponents. 'An element of proportionality' is certainly preferable to complete proportional representation. But it is like being 'a little bit pregnant.' It would lead to new parties in Parliament, minority government, and coalitions. If it did not, the true believers would not be satisfied. Proportional representation is wrong and we should have none of it. And, if you believe in it, why should you be content with only a third of seats allocated proportionally? 'An element of proportionality' risks being a contrivance to produce a particular result in a particular conjuncture.

Canada in Proportion

There is a special argument made in Canada for proportional representation. Regional differences have meant that some parties dominate in some parts of the country and are practically shut out in others. The Liberals, with the Parti Québécois (PQ), have been dominant in Quebec, and Reform, or the Tories, in Alberta. The Conservatives have been shut out in Quebec and the Liberals have held two seats or none in Alberta. Those who make the special case for proportional representation in Canada argue that our elections give a false representation of Canada, suggesting that there are no Conservatives in Quebec and only a handful of Liberals in Alberta, and that this false representation gives politicians with a strong regional bias too much influence, putting unnecessary strain on the nation.

One would have to be very stupid to think that because there were twenty-six Conservatives and only two Liberals elected in Alberta in 2004 there could have been only a handful of Liberals there, or to think that because there were no Conservatives elected in Quebec there were none there. The popular vote figures and the second-place finishes were all published. The recent history when Tories were elected in Quebec, when they swept the province twice in the eighties, is well known. Even after the 2008 election we know that there are 143,998 voters in

Alberta prepared to support a Liberal, and now the Tories have eleven seats in Quebec.

On the other hand, one would have to be almost as stupid to think that the difference of Alberta and the difference of Quebec were simply artefacts of the way we run our elections. Quebec *is* a place very different from the rest of Canada. There has been no secure Conservative base there in roughly a century. It would not have helped – might even have been a liability for the Conservatives – if they could have counted on electing a handful of members on less than 10 per cent of the vote in their lean years. Alberta too is different. It has been ready to elect Liberals when the Liberals listen, but too often the Liberals would not, and they might have been even less likely to listen if they could have counted on four or five seats from Alberta under proportional representation anyway.

Often electoral reform is proposed as a way of dealing with a problem arising in a specific political conjuncture. In a matter of years the problem and the argument for reform may disappear, but the reform, if adopted, will have produced new and unanticipated problems. Tom Flanagan, a long-time adviser to Stephen Harper, proposed adoption of the Australian Alternative Vote in Canada to get around the problem of the continuing Alliance / Progressive Conservatives rivalry.[37] Two years later the parties had merged. Had the Alternative Vote been adopted, they might still be with us, and that surely would not be a good thing.

Flanagan was also worried about Liberal dominance and the Conservatives being shut out of Quebec. After the 2006 election his concerns looked dated.

All Is for the Best

Election by plurality in single-member constituencies, or single member plurality voting (SMPV), as our present way of choosing MPs can be technically described – always remembering that it is not the device of a theory, but simply seemed the natural and obvious way from the start – tends to produce two competing parties as parties form in accordance with their purpose of forming a government or an alternative government. Canada has had third, fourth, and fifth parties because of regional strains. Even without them, history shows that there is no risk of two parties forming a duopoly. In Britain the Liberals declined and the Labour Party emerged. In several Canadian provinces United

Farmers, Progressives, Social Credit, the CCF, the Union National, the NDP, and the PQ broke in on apparently entrenched duopolies in a matter of years. In Ottawa the Reform Party came from nowhere to official opposition in a decade. SMPV is neither a barrier to serious new parties nor a protection for old parties. Rather, proportional representation perpetuates old parties in decline.

The huge change in British politics when Margaret Thatcher's Conservatives won the election of 1979 led to a brief anxiety that SMPV with its ability to produce a decisive change in government could produce another kind of instability. It looked at times in the eighties that Labour, seeming to move to the left, might get back into power and that Britain, having moved right under Thatcher, would lurch to the left on her defeat.

But it is not the effect of SMPV to produce lurches. The more common complaint, more properly a compliment, is that it produces a competition for the centre. The circumstances of 1979 were exceptional. Labour, captive to the big unions and subject to infiltration by the loony left, was unable to address Britain's problems as its better leaders would have. Cracks began to appear in the party, which led to the formation of the Social Democratic Party by breakaway Labour members. The postwar consensus of British politics was no longer effective but the Labour party could not move on. Only the Conservatives, coming to power after five years in opposition, had that freedom. By the time Labour returned to power in 1997 it had transformed itself and largely accepted the changes made under the Conservatives. There were no lurches.

The typical tendency of SMPV is to produce what was called Butskellism in Britain in the fifties. R.A.B. Butler, 'the best prime minister Britain never had,' was a long-serving centrist Conservative Cabinet minister, and Hugh Gaitskell was the moderate leader of the Labour Party in opposition from 1955 to 1963. Butskellism described the closeness of mainstream Conservative and Labour policies.

In Canada too, as in all countries whose elections are similar to ours, the main parties have historically competed for the mainstream. Only proportional representation rewards those whose positions can never command the support of more than a fraction of the voters.

4 Fun with Figures: The Paradox of Voting

Proportional representation is only one of many alternative ways of electing members of Parliament. Most tend to produce a more proportional representation of parties, but they do not necessarily assign seats to parties on the basis of party votes. Their proponents claim they more accurately and effectively express the voters' choices. This claim is made in ignorance or defiance of social choice theory and what is known as the paradox of voting.

And now we must deal with matters that may seem abstruse and academic but are fundamental to the understanding of voting.

About the time of the French Revolution, as voting began to seem important, the French mathematicians Borda and Condorcet discovered what came to be known as the paradox of voting. It can be simply illustrated in an example when three voters (1, 2, and 3) have to choose from three options or candidates (A, B, and C) by a preferential ballot:

1	2	3
A	B	C
B	C	A
C	A	B

What do we find? A majority (1 and 3) prefer A to B. A majority (1 and 2) prefer B to C. So we can eliminate C and choose A and B or have a runoff between them? No! Because a majority (2 and 3) prefer C to A.

If an individual said he preferred A to B and B to C and C to A, we would say that he could not make up his mind. But this paradox lurks in all voting where there are more than two choices, in all the schemes intended to improve our elections. There is no issue when there are only two choices. There will be a majority for one, and a majority is accepted. All alternative election schemes claim to enable voters to choose rationally and effectively from more than two options. But faced with more than two choices, as the paradox of voting illustrates, the people may not be able to make up their mind. They may not know what they want.

The paradox of voting was forgotten until the 1860s when Charles Dodgson, the Oxford mathematician who wrote *Alice in Wonderland* under the pseudonym Lewis Carroll, rediscovered it and wrestled with various schemes to overcome it. Again it was largely forgotten until the middle of the last century when the economists Duncan Black and Kenneth Arrow made the most systematic exploration of its implications.

In 1951 Arrow published his general possibility theorem, which, by mathematics I do not pretend to follow and will not reproduce, proved that 'there is no method of voting which will remove the paradox of voting ... no matter how complicated.'[38]

Economists have argued about the importance of Arrow's theorem and his proof has been reworked but it has never been refuted. It was cited as the basis of his Nobel Prize in economics. There is a considerable literature in political science following Black and Arrow's work but, oddly, the bulk of academic, government, and popular writing about electoral reform simply ignores it.

The failure of the proponents of electoral reform to advert to the paradox of voting, even long enough to dismiss it, can only be explained by their being like the promoters of perpetual motion machines, so wrapped up in the details of their invention, and blinded by the wonders it will perform, that they must ignore that what they are attempting is impossible.

The paradox of voting usually surprises people. They are discomfited that mathematics should intrude so unhelpfully into politics. But it should not be surprising. All the paradox of voting does is confirm that, where there is no majority, a majority cannot be contrived by summing up preferences or voting in stages or any other trick of electoral reform.

People tend to think it can be done because they imagine politics is all what Duncan Black called single-peaked preferences. A single-peaked preference describes the graph that results when, across a range of choices, the voters' choices always show a single peak with the second, third, and further preferences falling away to the side or sides. The classic example is the left/right political spectrum. If we imagine that all there is to politics is where you stand from left to right, then any voter from far left to far right with moderate left and right and centrist in between will have preferences with a single peak somewhere along the way from left to right. Duncan Black showed that when voters' preferences are single peaked, the paradox of voting is practically eliminated.

To return to our original simple example to illustrate the idea of a single-peaked preference, if A were left, B centrist, and C right, and where one stood from left to right was all that mattered, no one would have the preference C, A, B. Such a voter would be a right-winger preferring a left winger over a centrist for his second preference. In fact politics is not a simple question of left, right, and centre. It is often difficult to know what is left and what is right. Politics is multidimensional. In Canada, for instance, many voters have switched between the CCF or NDP and the Conservatives and never voted Liberal. In France the working-class vote has often been in play between the Communists and the far right National Front with the moderate parties hardly getting a look in. However distasteful we may find some voters' choices, we cannot simply put them down to ignorance or confusion and arrange our elections assuming that there are only single-peaked preferences. Politics no more than life can proceed in one dimension.

The paradox of voting does not mean that voting is pointless or democracy impossible. It means that we must understand what voting can do and how democracy can be effective. Elections are proceedings to allow voters to decide who will govern. They are not simply an occasion for people to say what they would like. They are not an opinion survey. They must, if they are to serve their purpose, produce a decision. Our present elections do that. How people vote decides who will govern. Once the votes are counted we know who will govern.

The paradox of voting is an instance of a difficulty with all voting procedures. When there are two choices and one choice wins by 51 per cent to 49 per cent, it is only by convention that we can say that the people have chosen that one. Fifty-one per cent have chosen that one and the other 49 per cent must just lump it. Voting procedures are ways of producing decisions, where they must and will be made, as in government. The true people's choice, unanimity, is almost always impossible. So a majority, or failing that a plurality, will have to do. It is a result and the most popular possible. Accepting a plurality of 37 per cent is no more arbitrary or unfair than accepting a majority. A voting procedure must produce a result and be sensitive to changes in people's judgments. Only our present way of voting does and is.

Voters can, as things stand in Canada, choose a government and, if they are not satisfied with it, kick it out. All alternative election systems take that choice away from voters by attempting to capture the will of voters without eliciting a decision on government. That decision is then made in obscure bargaining over which the voters have no control.

There is nothing evidently compelling about a majority except that it is necessarily the most popular result. Where there are more than two choices, a majority may be unobtainable, but a plurality produces a result and, like a majority when it can be found, the most popular.

Champions of electoral reform like to sum up the votes of opposition parties, usually close to 60 per cent, and attempt to deny legitimacy to a government that a large majority voted against. But votes for parties that do not form a government cannot be construed simply as votes against the party that does. If voters were simply concerned with whether the Liberals, for example, should form the government, then a majority that did not want them to could easily enough vote for the non-Liberal candidate most likely to win and at least hold the Liberals to a minority. If the non-Liberal MPs elected truly reflected the wishes of their voters as we are premising them, they could support an alternative minority government or form a coalition. But most voters are voting for something and against perhaps more than one alternative. So Conservative and New Democrat voters will vote for their candidates, at the risk of letting the Liberal in, and their votes cannot simply be totted up as votes against the Liberals. If voters really were thinking 'Anyone but the Liberals,' then they should have voted accordingly, as I suggest. It is a fault of electoral reform that it makes voting against difficult or impossible.

All the voters can do is choose representatives and hold them accountable at elections. Our election procedures were not founded on theory but practically, to make government answerable to the voters – and to produce practical results.

The British Columbia Scheme

Many electoral schemes are proposed as in some way better reflecting the will of the voters, whether tending to produce proportional representation of parties or not. None of them work, in the sense either that they give voters more control over government, or that they overcome the paradox of voting because, as Arrow demonstrated, that cannot be done. To illustrate this it is best to examine the single transferable vote as proposed by the British Columbia Citizens' Assembly. It came closest to being adopted in Canada. Its seductive elaboration represents the reformist urge at its most obstinate and obtuse. The very highest claims have been made for it. Keen students of electoral reform have called it a cult.[39]

It works like this: ridings would elect more than one member. We shall suppose, for example, that in the riding of Fraser three members are to be elected. Voters would be asked to mark an order of preference among the candidates on their ballot. The number of ballots is divided by the number of members to be elected plus one, and the next full number above that is the 'Droop quota,' the number of votes needed to elect a member. We shall imagine that there are 10,000 ballots. Therefore 2,501 votes are need to elect a member.

If a candidate gets 2,501 or more first-preference votes she is declared elected. If she gets more than 2,501 votes, say 3,000, then a transfer value is calculated for her second preferences by dividing the surplus votes by her total number of votes. So her second preferences are transferred at a value of 499/3000.

If no candidate gets 2,501 votes, the candidate with the least votes is eliminated, and the second preferences on the ballots on which she was the first preference are counted. The process of transferring votes goes on until three candidates have got 2,501 votes and are declared elected. Votes for eliminated candidates can be transferred several times at full value if they do not land with a winning candidate, and surplus votes for winning candidates can be transferred at ever-smaller fractions. The arithmetic elaboration of the single transferable vote encourages the hope that it makes every vote count, even when all but a handful of experts have lost track of what is happening to the votes.

Why are there to be three members elected in the riding of Fraser? STV supporters are torn on the size of ridings. They could not make up their minds in British Columbia. The theoretical ideal would be to make the whole province, or country, one big riding, but even a five-member riding requires a dangerously long ballot. And STV supporters hope to persuade the voters that they will still have a local representative, but that becomes harder as the ridings get bigger. Examples usually use figures such as I have with a neat 10,000 voters. But the seven-member ridings contemplated in British Columbia would have had upwards of 200,000 voters.

STV needs multi-member ridings because it is a contrivance to allow the election of members by a small percentage of the voters. The bigger the riding, the smaller the Droop quota and the percentage of votes needed to elect a member. While the percentage of voters needed to elect a member declines, the number of members ostensibly elected to represent voters who do not support them, even vehemently oppose them, rises.

They say the voters of Fraser elect three members, but an individual voter is only, at best, electing one. Once a voter's preferences have 'counted' towards the election of one member they are cast aside. Any other member elected in the riding no more represents that voter than the member for Halifax represents a voter in Whitehorse. It is not a question of whether the voter likes or would have voted for that other member. He could not, no more than a voter in Halifax can, vote for the member for Whitehorse. He may have placed the other member somewhere on his list of preferences, but that preference would not have been counted.

All the candidates' names are on the ballot, but the voter does not get to choose three candidates to fill the three seats. If the first-preference candidate, the one with the real vote, is elected, the ballot may be cast aside. Conversely, it is possible to fill in all preferences so that, literally, the last person you would want elected wins your vote.

STV makes a show of seeking the voters' will in exhaustive detail, but it is a contrivance designed to restrict the voters' say to what STV deems a fair share. STV may seem to ask which three would you like to see elected, but it is really only asking which one.

The transfer of votes to second and further preferences is intended to avoid 'wasted' votes. Leaving aside those whose votes never count for a winning candidate, who may be almost 25 per cent of the voters in a three-member riding, there will also be a great number of wasted preferences, if voters use them all, as they are encouraged to do. The voter who conscientiously decides between the Monster Raving Loony Party and the Natural Law Party for his nineteenth preference will be wasting his time. The greater part of preferences may never even be counted and recorded. At least under our present system every vote is counted and recorded.

Conversely, anything between 25 per cent and 49 per cent support for a party – assuming, as in the end STV proponents do, that voters will follow party lines – makes no difference. Forty-nine per cent Tory, 26 per cent Liberal, and 25 per cent New Democrat will elect one member for each party, as will 25 per cent Tory, 37 per cent Liberal, and 38 per cent New Democrat, or 25 per cent plus one for each, with 25 per cent minus three for the also-rans. This insensitivity to differences in the vote can be reduced by increasing the number of members to be elected. If seven are to be elected, 12.5 per cent will elect one member and 38 per cent will elect three. But the more members to be elected and the

larger the riding, the longer the ballot becomes and the more unreal the
pretence that voters are making an informed choice among candidates.
Better to go for straightforward proportional representation and ask
each voter to choose a list, leaving the details of who gets in to the party.

STV is strongly sold as a means of achieving proportional representation but pretends to offer the best of both worlds by asking voters
to choose between individuals. Independents could well win. What it
really does is allow the election of members with a small fraction of the
vote. In a riding with ten members, just over 9 per cent of the vote would
be enough. It is complained in our present elections that members are
elected with as little as 30 per cent of the vote. 'How can they speak for
their riding?' it is asked. Still more can it be asked how a member who
got less than 10 per cent of the vote can speak for the riding.

While STV is presented as keen to express the voter's will, it strictly
controls its expression. The riding of Mackenzie elects six members. But
in practice the voter can only choose one. Once her vote has elected one
member, the choice of the other five is out of her hands. If 85 per cent of
the voters do not want to be represented by a nutbar who can get 15 per
cent of the votes, there is nothing they can do about it.

While barring the voter from the effective choice of all the members
who are to represent her, STV asks for a range of choices that is unreal.
The preference of the Liberal voter between the New Democrats and
the Conservatives and then between the individual New Democrat
and Conservative candidates may be contrived but cannot be serious.
It may be mischievous. Voters evidently have some difficulty deciding how to cast a single vote. Their choice of multiple preferences of
decreasing value must become meaningless.

When I vote I want only my candidate to win. Even that is not an
easy decision. Depending on the circumstances, I could work out some
kind of tactical preference among the other candidates, if obliged to,
but generally a second, third, or fourth preference would be a contrivance meaning far less than my real vote. If there were a fascist or communist threat, I should want to do whatever I could to vote against it,
but STV would not let me. A preferential ballot asks for far more choice
than voters can seriously make – and no votes against. Any vote may
become a vote for a candidate at full value.

Electoral Perversity

Despite its mathematical sophistication, STV can produce perverse
results. Most startlingly, it can breach monotonicity, the surely basic

principle that a candidate should be better off it he or she gets more votes. That this is not, as it should be, necessarily so, can most simply be illustrated with an example from STV's little cousin, the alternative vote, where voters electing a single member fill out a preferential ballot and the candidate with the lowest vote is eliminated until one candidate gets 50 per cent of the votes.

Suppose there are three candidates and twenty-one voters with the following preferences:

	1st	2nd	3rd
7	A	B	C
3	B	A	C
5	B	C	A
6	C	A	B

On first preferences B gets eight votes, A gets seven, and C six. With the lowest number of votes, C is eliminated, and those who had C as their first preference having A as their second, on the second count A wins:

13	A
8	B

Suppose the three voters whose preference was B, A, C had switched to A, B, C:

	1st	2nd	3rd
7	A	B	C
3	A	B	C
5	B	C	A
6	C	A	B

Now B has the lowest number of votes on the first count and is eliminated. The B voters' second choice being C, on the second count A loses and C wins:

10	A
11	C

More votes for A, and no more votes for C, lead to A losing. It can also happen that a shift of votes between two candidates makes no difference to them but may cause one or more other candidates, whose votes remain the same, to win or lose.

STV's supporters say this rarely, if ever, happens. How can they know? One would have to demonstrate that in any given election no candidate could have been better placed with fewer or lower preferences. One would have to count all the preferences, which, in practice, is not done.

If indeed it rarely happens, it is because, unlike the cheerful free-for-all depicted in STV propaganda, with voters casting their preferences across party lines, STV elections are run by the parties and for most voters the only preferences counted are between the candidates of one party and those in a party-inspired pecking order.

STV's elaboration suggests that it captures the voter's will with great precision, but only if the voter's will is precisely cut to STV's theory. Voting in a three-member riding, Mary lists the three Suede Party candidates 1, 2, and 3. STV registers a preference in that order. Very likely Mary has no preference among them, at least none between 1 and 2 or 2 and 3. The preference STV registers is an artefact. But it may be enough to elect 1 before the preferences of others who strongly prefer 2 to 1 come into play. Mary did not mean to give 1 an advantage over 2 but she did. Or 3 may be the one Suede candidate with a chance but be eliminated before Mary's third preference is counted. As the counting goes on, things become even more tricky. She means, voting 'sincerely' as STV wants her to do, that she prefers 4 to all the others left in the race. But when Mary's fourth preference is counted, the real contest is between her 6 and 7, and 7 is elected while 4 is eliminated.

STV claims by its contrivance and mathematics more effectively to express the will of the voters than any other system. In the end, all that can be said is that STV produces the result that STV produces. When it can be demonstrated that STV gets the will of the voters wrong, that more votes can lose a candidate an election, STV's claims are demonstrated to be false.

Single-Member Plurality Voting Rules! OK

Single-member plurality voting is riddled with faults for the theorists. But to find those faults you have to accept their theories.

Obviously SMPV does not produce proportional representation. It was not supposed to and we should not want it to. It came before there were parties, and parties grew up to perform a function in a Parliament so elected – a function they cannot perform under proportional representation.

SMPV does not produce a majority winner, but the paradox of voting shows that a majority winner may not be possible with more than two candidates. Systems designed always to produce an apparently majority winner, like the alternative vote, may produce perverse results. At least with SMPV, another vote for a candidate can only help that candidate, while with preference ballots it may not.

Voting procedures can be analysed under several mathematical schemes. But that way lies madness. Condorcet rankings, Borda counts, Copeland scores may conflict. A candidate eliminated under STV may have been the second choice of most voters and would have won on a Borda count, which assigns points for preferences, four for first preference, three for second, and so on. Or a candidate elected under STV may have a lower Condorcet ranking than one eliminated, that is, the eliminated candidate may be preferred by most voters to the one elected.

Each scheme is valid only on its own terms and none can be shown to produce the 'right' result. None overcomes the paradox of voting. SMPV may fail by any one of the schemes or produce the 'right' result by them all.

STV, like other alternative electoral systems including proportional representation, produces a result, it coughs up so many MPs, but it is not a decision. All the differences among the voters and their own indecision is carried forward unresolved; it fixes on them. It fails the purpose of an election, which is to let the voters decide. And beyond the backroom bargaining, for which no one can be held accountable, what may emerge from an elected assembly divided several ways is itself subject to the paradox of voting and the impossibility of aggregating preferences, control of agenda, or logrolling.

It will be said that we do not always get a decision as it is. The federal elections of 23 January 2006 and 14 October 2008 produced minority governments. The voters may be genuinely undecided, even when SMPV offers them a chance to decide. With only two parties in contention, the result may be so close as to be practically a tie. But parties do not disagree on everything. A minority government can govern for a year or two, getting a good deal done. The 2006 election was decisive, producing a historic change in government. And where regional differences produce a party like the Bloc Québécois that holds back and is kept apart from the government of the country, there is an inevitable problem that no electoral system can avoid. If proportional representation reduced the Bloc's number of seats, it would also increase its bargaining power in a further divided House.

But with SMPV the voters, and the candidates, know exactly what happens with a vote. Under any other procedure, preferences may come into play or not, and at an arbitrary value that the voter cannot understand or control. A voter under SMPV who votes for a candidate with no hope of winning knows what he is doing. He is neither wasting his vote nor throwing it away. If he cared which of the front-runners won, he could vote for that candidate. He prefers not to.

SMPV asks voters to decide and permits voters to decide. Other voting procedures suborn indecision.

Proponents of electoral reform have a one-sided perspective on elections. They see only the voters, and for them an election is about producing as exact as possible a reproduction of the notions and wishes of the voters. But elections are a procedure for making decisions, on who will represent us and, indirectly, who will govern and how, and for making government responsible to the voters. Elections have two sides: the voters and the candidates. It is the interaction between these in elections that produces democratic government. If elections simply produce a small-scale model of the electorate, they decide nothing. All schemes for electoral reform aim futilely at this stasis. Our present way of voting, arising pragmatically over the centuries, produces a dynamic interaction between the candidates and parties, seeking the widest possible support, and voters judging the candidates and parties not simply on their own thoughts, sentiments, and interests, but on the breadth of their appeal and their ability to lead, persuade and govern effectively.

The sometimes shambolic free-for-all nominations we know, dominated by instant party members, leave much to be desired, but at least they involve some popular and local participation. With large ridings under STV or lists under proportional representation, whatever show of grass-roots participation the parties might put on, the candidates would be chosen by the party apparatus.

Making a show of nuanced and disinterested understanding, some academics suggest that different electoral systems may suit different countries and different political cultures. As the arguments for all the contrived electoral systems are abstract and technical, this is implausible. All that is true is that bad electoral systems may be less bad, depending on circumstances. Ireland copes with STV because it is a small country. A five-member constituency has only about 100,000 voters, no more than some Canadian ridings. And whatever the faults of a country's political institution, a political culture will develop to make them work as far as possible. These things argue against change in Canada. It is not a small country. And its political culture is adapted to our present way of voting.

5 The People Speak? British Columbia's Citizens' Assembly

A referendum was held on the STV at the same time as the British Columbia general election of 17 May 2005. The referendum rules required a 60 per cent yes vote for the result to be binding. The yes vote was only 57 per cent. A second referendum held with the general election of 12 May 2009 yielded a 60 per cent vote against STV. The history of how British Columbia came to vote on the STV is instructive.

British Columbia had adopted the alternative vote for the elections of 1952 and 1953 for the express purpose of keeping the CCF out of power while preserving the Liberals and the Conservatives, who had been in a coalition. The alternative vote, while maintaining single-member ridings, asked voters to express their preference among the candidates. Liberals could make Conservatives their second choice, and Conservatives Liberals, in the hope of keeping out the CCF.

The result was the collapse of the Liberals and Conservatives and the emergence of Social Credit under the former Conservative W.A.C. Bennett, who promptly dropped the alternative vote. In the 2001 general election, the resurrected Liberals promised a new era for British Columbia, including a citizens' assembly on electoral reform.

A citizens' assembly is a procedure intended to delude voters that their fellow citizens have spontaneously and disinterestedly come up with measures for the public good that deserve respect because of their ostensibly popular origin. In fact STV was the practically intended and predictable outcome of the citizens' assembly process.

The government had handed the task of designing the citizens' assembly process to Gordon Gibson, a fervent supporter of the STV. Immediately after its report was published, he was celebrating its recommendation of STV as the work of 'ordinary folk' with a 'legitimate parentage.'[40]

The formal terms of reference of the citizens' assembly left it open to it to recommend that the existing electoral system be continued. No one believed that it would. The citizens' assembly's job was reform, and those who set it up and ran it were determined to have it.

The organizers of the citizens' assembly went to elaborate lengths to assure that it was representative in a pictorial sense. Gender and age balance was assiduously pursued, though after a special effort to reduce the proportion of the spry retired who were willing to serve, and to round up youth, those age cohorts remained respectively over and under represented. As the voters lists used by the organizers did not specify religion, race, and other categories, they could do nothing about them, but contrived correct Aboriginal representation.

A remote connection with politics was a disqualification from sitting in the assembly and, so far as could be detected, none of its members had ever sullied themselves in politics. At least indifference to, and even ignorance of, the activity with which they were to concern themselves was sought. All this was designed to give the citizens' assembly a spurious moral authority. Politicians, it was supposed, would design or advise a scheme for their political advantage. It is widely suspected that politicians are resistant to reform for selfish reasons. I write because this is not true. Politicians are all too keen on or receptive to reform.

Two hundred voters were randomly selected from each of the seventy-nine ridings in British Columbia. Because of poor responses to a first mailing, and a desire to even out age cohorts, further draws had to be conducted, and the 15,800 finally became over 23,000. From these, 964 self-selected themselves by attending meetings, at which another 50 dropped out. Less than 4 per cent of those invited to participate chose to offer themselves. The 158 members of the assembly were randomly selected from these. The most important factor in deciding who got on the assembly was the choice of individuals to take on a part-time job, at $150 a day, mostly weekends. A propensity to speculate on changes to 'the system' and a suspicion of the way politics is done, would stimulate interest. Where they were lacking, vacant curiosity or earnest willingness to learn would do. The 'let well enough alone' school was predictably under-represented.

Only 6 pages of the 20-page *Final Report*[41] of the citizens' assembly, sent to all British Columbia voters, describe and make extravagant claims for the STV the assembly decided on. This is meagre for such a complicated system. The 280-page *Technical Report*[42] devotes, at a generous count, only 15 pages to explaining and promoting the STV. The rest is devoted to describing how the citizens' assembly was chosen and went about its work. Thirty-four pages describe how it was chosen. Fifty-three pages simply list the names of those who made submissions. Two pages show furniture arrangements for the public meetings. Evidently, those running the assembly thought that the elaborate show they put on would be most effective in persuading the voters to accept the result.

Perhaps they thought that detailed arguments were more than the voters could be expected to cope with. But if they were that technical and challenging, how could their proxies in the citizens' assembly come to grips with them in little more than twenty days of meetings, much of which was taken up with listening to prolix and repetitive presentations? It is indeed unlikely that members of the assembly did fully understand what they were doing. How many could explain the weighted inclusive Gregory method for allocating so-called surplus votes. They had to take the virtue of STV on faith in the experts, and the hope was that the voters would take it on faith in the assembly.

If it had really been intended that the citizens' assembly should come up with its own answer, it would have been given a deadline and a budget and told to go to work as it saw fit. Instead, the assembly's work was rigorously planned and directed. They were softened up by academics talking at them and guided by staff at every stage to the predictable outcome. It came down to a choice between STV and something like German proportional representation, with STV favoured 123 to 31. On a final vote, all but 7 came on side in favour of recommending STV in a referendum.

So, in a few weekends, a group of people who were not supposed to have thought much about it before were persuaded to toss aside election procedures developed and used over centuries and over much of the democratic world and to replace them with the most complex and technical system ever devised.

The academic experts on election systems were all biased in favour of change. People do not spend years studying election systems in their dry detail only to say it is all a waste of time and our present way of voting works fine. Political scientists who do think that have looked at the question and moved on to other subjects. The assembly's principal academic resource, David Farrell, of the University of Manchester, is a proponent of STV. He writes and speaks in measured academic tones calculated to assure authority for his convictions.

The public hearings were equally biased. According to a survey conducted for the assembly, 95.6 per cent of those at the public hearings wanted a change in the electoral system.

On the assembly's vast website, the keys to understanding voting – the paradox of voting, Kenneth Arrow, Duncan Black, the impossibility theorem, Borda and Condorcet – either do not appear or are buried in a few of the hundreds of submissions that most assembly members will have neither heard nor read.

A citizens' assembly remains a popular marketing scheme for reform. Ontario has gone down the same road. Gordon Gibson[43] and the *Globe and Mail*'s Ottawa columnist John Ibbitson[44] have suggested a national citizens' assembly to deal with everything, an elected Senate, electoral reform – everything I attack in this book. But its faults should be evident.

Truly left to its own, it would likely produce confusion, acrimony, and stalemate – a shambles. Instructed, like British Columbia's, it is a sham. It is not representative because it must finally be self-selected, and it is not responsible because it just vanishes away.

The whole citizens' assembly process was an elaborate show designed to persuade voters that they were, in the subsequent referendum, simply being asked to confirm what they had themselves, through the citizens' assembly, devised. If the citizens' assembly had been truly representative of the voters, it would not have voted overwhelmingly for a proposal that 42 per cent of the voters, despite relentless propaganda, and no organized opposition, rejected.

The assembly's work completed, on schedule, and a new electoral system recommended, as expected, a final report, tendentiously entitled *Making Every Vote Count: The Case for Electoral Reform in British Columbia*, was submitted to the attorney general and sent to everyone in the province. The parties had agreed to keep silent on the referendum question and were in any case caught up in the extended election campaign encouraged by a fixed election date. Referendum legislation elaborately restricted campaigning, and few people bothered to address their fellow voters on the referendum question. The field was left open to the assembly's shameless and unqualified propaganda, written, like all the assembly's publications, by its enthusiastic staff. A series of wild claims were made for STV:[45]

- *It is easy to use*: This was said pre-emptively precisely because, with its lengthy and complicated ballot, it is not easy to use. The report repeatedly boldly claims the opposite of the truth. It claims that bigger ridings strengthen local representation. It claims that there are no safe seats under STV when seats where only one sixth of the votes assure election are actually safer than existing single-member ridings.
- *It gives fairer results*: STV tends to produce more proportional representation, but saying it is fairer begs the question of what is fair about proportional representation.
- *It gives more power to voters … All candidates must work hard to earn every vote*: This is the exact opposite of the truth. Under STV, candidates are interested only in their quota and have no incentive to pursue the majority of voters. Only under SMPV does, for the candidate, 'every vote count.'
- *It gives greater voter choice … Choosing more than one member*: Again untrue. Anyone who understands STV knows that, under it, each voter gets to elect only one member, if that, however many are to be elected in the riding. Most preferences will never be counted, and it is in the hands of other voters who will fill the other seats.

The report returns again and again to STV's tendency to produce proportional representation while claiming that it will reduce the hold of parties on politics. In practice, parties run the elections under STV and assure that they get the best results the system allows. The report imagines voters gaily distributing their preferences across three or more parties and claims, on no basis of experience or logic, that politics under STV would be less partisan and more civil. It wants to have it both ways: downplaying parties, party loyalty, party discipline, and partisanship while rewarding parties with seats for votes because in proportional representation's blinkered perspective that is what 'fairness' means.

STV's relationship with proportional representation is complicated. Because it allows members to be elected with a small minority of the vote, what it was designed to do by Thomas Hare in the nineteenth century, it does allow smaller parties to elect members. But proportionality is restricted by the practical restriction on riding sizes. And with a preferential ballot what are seats to be proportional to? To first preferences or all preferences, most of which will never be counted.

Trying to answer the question reveals that either STV's claim to offer a cornucopia of choice or its claim to achieve proportionality must be wrong.

Enough British Columbia voters were unpersuaded to deny STV the level of approval required by the referendum law. One more push, with voters better 'educated,' said the disappointed advocates of STV, and in 2009 we'll get there. It was not to be.

6 How to Vote: Some Simple Ways

The complexity of the STV is a futile attempt to capture the imagined will of the voters while preventing them from deciding anything. Our present way of voting is beautifully simple, produces a decision, and is sensitive to changes in voter choices. Tactical voting is simple, even desirable, and its effects are predictable.

Many reformers worry about tactical voting. They argue that we should be able to vote 'sincerely' for whoever we think best and that if the electoral system forces us to consider whether such 'sincere' voting will produce the best outcome it is faulty. They seek 'sincere' elections in which we vote for exactly what we want and see the result in government. It is a delusion.

What is meant by tactical voting? A common contemporary example is a New Democrat who, fearful of a Conservative victory, votes for a Liberal as the one most likely to defeat the Conservative. What is wrong with that? How is it insincere? The voter sincerely fears the Conservatives, sincerely hopes the New Democrats will see better days, and sincerely chooses the Liberal as the best option in the circumstances.

The reformer's idea of sincerity is too strict. For the reformer, the only sincere vote is one cast with wholehearted, doubt-free, unqualified enthusiasm. By the reformer's standard the only sincere vote I have ever cast was the one I cast for myself, even though I knew that I could not win and my efforts as a candidate likely only resulted in the defeat of the sitting Liberal and the election of the New Democrat to Queen's Park, where he sits still twenty years later. With every other vote I have cast I have been unhappy with the candidate, the party, the leader, the platform, or all of them, but I judged I was doing the right thing in voting as I did. I would not start a Pepall Party to get everything right. I vote the best I can in the circumstances, like any tactical voter. So do we all, according to our lights.

All voters must accept that there is no perfect choice. The only people who can vote with perfect enthusiasm – the reformer's measure of sincerity – are pure partisans who identify themselves with a party without concern for what it is doing or may do. Such voters, like die-hard Leafs fans, may always be with us, but they cannot be the model voters of reform.

Even when there are several parties or candidates to choose from, a sensible voter will make his choice of the best, all things considered, including the prospect of getting elected and being effective in government. He need not be so pessimistic as to see his choice as the best of a bad lot, but even if he is prepared to give his loyalty to a party or candidate, over many elections or for life, he will be a realist and conscious of how far short his choice is from his ideal. The tactical voter does the same, and there is nothing wrong in principle with that and no reason why an electoral system should be designed to discourage it. Rather, it should encourage voters to make the best practical use of their votes, according to their lights. The tactical situation should always be considered.

In practice, tactical voting may be a mistake. The voter may be mistaken about the strength of the parties or the candidates. In Canada at least, she is likely unduly alarmed at the prospect of victory of whichever party she is seeking by tactical voting to defeat. But she is doing her best to achieve the best result according to her lights, and more power to her. Any vote may be a mistake. No electoral regime can keep people from making mistakes.

How much tactical voting there is, nobody knows. The concept on examination becomes unclear. The picture of the staunch New Democrat, sick at heart, voting for a Liberal while quaking in fear of the Conservatives is implausible. The stauncher the New Democrat, the less likely he is to see much to choose between the Liberals and the Conservatives. If he allows Liberal attacks on the Conservatives to sway him, he must give the Liberals more credence than a staunch New Democrat should. What passes for tactical voting is more likely a floating voter who would be prepared to give the New Democrats a chance if they were serious contenders but likes the Liberals well enough.

Obviously many voters vote for a candidate they know cannot win. For supporters of proportional representation, until the glorious day of proportionality comes, they are wasting their votes. The implication is that they should at least try to make their vote count by voting for a candidate who may win. But such voters are voting strategically. They know their party cannot win this time in this election, but by voting for its candidate anyway they prepare the ground for a future victory. Such were the 275,000 who voted Reform in 1988. They did not care for the Progressive Conservatives, the Liberals, or the New Democrats. STV's demand that they express a preference among those they would have preferred not to see elected might take a third or fourth preference as a full vote, perhaps carrying a candidate over the quota and into a seat.

Looked at another way, the tactical voter is simply trying to choose a government, and our present way of voting, uniquely, allows the voter to do that.

No alternative electoral system actually overcomes what reformers see as the tactical voting problem. Pure, strict, proportional representation comes closest only to the extent that it attenuates the control of the voter over the government so far as to make tactical calculation fruitless. But tactical voting occurs under proportional representation. In Germany, Christian Democrats voted for Free Democrats to keep them as a viable coalition partner.

In more elaborate electoral systems, like STV, tactical calculations become more difficult as the actual effect of the multiple preferences becomes obscure. Voters simply cannot follow the consequences of their votes. But for those who can follow them, they can become sinister. Preferences can be used to promote opposition candidates who will be trouble for their own party or to skew the order in which candidates will be eliminated for tactical advantage. These are insincere votes indeed – not votes cast for the best candidate likely to win but possibly the worst candidate or the candidate least likely to win, because the complicated working of the STV just might reward such perversity. In the 2007 Irish election, the opposition leader was encouraging voters to support minor party candidates with no hope of winning in the hope it would help his party.[46] Whether it did his party any good we cannot know. He lost anyway.

Though difficult, such tactical voting under STV can hardly be blamed by advocates of a system that asks voters to express preferences among numerous candidates they do not like – preferences that may end up being counted as full votes for them.

The only protection against perverse tactical voting is the almost incalculable and chaotic working of STV. As we have seen, a slight shift in preferences between two candidates in a multi-member riding may make no difference to the result for either of those candidates but change the result for several other candidates because of its effect on the order in which they are eliminated. A shift in preference against a candidate may even result in her election.

Voting for Individuals: Representatives

All democracies are necessarily representative. We choose individuals to make laws and govern for us. We cannot do it ourselves. How can we best choose representatives?

In our elections the candidate who gets the most votes in each riding gets to represent us. It seems so obvious and sensible. Through much of history and over much of the world that has been how it worked, and people have been content with it. Unprompted by the reformers' argument that it is unfair, most people would probably still be content with it.

Making the candidate who gets the most votes the MP is not just a random way of deciding who should represent us, like drawing lots. The most votes is the best criterion of the representativeness of the candidate. And it is a criterion that will impel the candidate to be representative. The candidate who gets the most votes has the best claim to represent the generality of voters. The candidate seeking the most votes must seek them as widely as possible. For the candidate, at least, in the phrase favoured by reformers, every vote counts.

And as long as every vote counts in that way, as candidates seek every vote, as members assiduously cultivate their constituents, every voter has some influence whether his vote actually elects a member or not. All candidates want his vote. Under STV or proportional representation, candidates or parties are interested only in their pool of voters.

Reformers have a faulty understanding of democratic representation. They think Parliament should represent the people as a painting represents a scene, in all its hues and shapes. They think that all the theories or interests, issues or cultures, genders or age groups that could be found in a survey should be reproduced directly, with the faithfulness of a magic realist painting, through an election in which it is enough to get a fraction of the votes marshalled around a theory or interest, an issue or ethnicity or whatever, to get elected.

STV encourages what the nineteenth-century English political writer Walter Bagehot called voluntary constituencies.[47] Criticizing the original version of what developed into the STV, Bagehot contrasted what he called compulsory constituencies with voluntary constituencies. Compulsory constituencies are the geographically defined ridings in which we vote, with the most popular candidate winning. As Bagehot pointed out, under reform proposals, voters could, as it were, voluntarily form their own constituencies to elect a member to their liking. Under STV, any group of voters large enough to reach the Droop quota can elect a member, regardless of the preferences of the rest of the voters. In practice, it is parties that do this work. The member so chosen neither intends nor is intended to represent all or most voters, but only those who chose her. So elected, she would be expected and impelled to serve not the country but the interest or cause that put her in Parliament. In practice, it is parties that constitute these voluntary constituencies, but there is a serious risk that ethnic or racial blocs could form under STV.

But it is not the role of MPs to represent voters in that way, to be as it were a random sample of the people. And it is not the role of government to serve the people divided in their theories or interests, issues or cultures, genders or age groups, and so on. Government has to do with the common interest and affairs of the people. MPs must concern themselves with the commonweal and must try to represent voters in their common concerns and not as they may be divided. They are best able to represent us if they seek and get the most votes. If they only seek and get the less than 15 per cent of the vote needed to get elected in a six-member STV riding, they may not even be able to represent that less than 15 per cent, because they have not had to concern themselves with the commonweal.

In electing a member of Parliament we are choosing a person to serve us, just as we do when we elect a mayor. A candidate's party affiliation may generally be an overwhelming factor in our choice, but it does not follow that we are simply voting for a party. We are not. The advocates of proportional representation attempt to obscure that fact with their emphasis on parties. Their comparisons of the popular vote for candidates of the various parties with the number of seats they win are misleading. Voters are not voting for parties and, if forced to by proportional representation, would vote differently.

It is assumed in most discussions of elections that voters, practically speaking, just vote for a party. Opinion polls are conducted on this assumption. A fair proportion of voters may not know who the candidates are when they cast their votes, or at least anything about them, attending only to the party affiliation now shown on ballots. But if voters are so in thrall to parties, it is a puzzle how independents like Chuck Cadman and John Nunziata can ever be elected.

Proponents of different voting procedures suggest that parties somehow get in the way of voters choosing the individual they would like best to represent them. But elections are not simply popularity contests. They would hardly work well if people simply voted for the person they would most like to meet at a barbecue. Polls sometimes show 'approval ratings' and other questions designed to elicit the popularity of leaders apart from their party. What the candidates' politics may be must be a dominating factor, and the parties roughly identify them with a brand name. If the party label, however, were all that mattered, a lot that goes on in politics would be inexplicable. Why do parties seek star candidates if candidates do not matter? Why do incumbents relentlessly curry favour with voters if all that will matter on election day is their party affiliation?

Some political scientists, too keen on abstract analysis, see our elections as performing two distinct functions that may conflict: electing a representative and choosing a government. They imagine voters in a quandary where a candidate they admire runs for a party they revile, or vice versa. The real world is different. If candidate Galahad is standing for the Dodgy Party, voters will either think Galahad is not such a shining knight after all or his party not so dodgy if he is prepared to stand for it. If candidate Mordred is standing for the Party of Angels, they will think Mordred may not be so bad or will be kept in line by the Angels, or the Angels have fallen.

Voters may greatly admire an individual without either wanting him as their MP, or a government formed from his party. They may think nothing of an individual but think he will make an adequate MP, better at least than the alternatives. Voters make their judgments after much thought or little, ignorantly or studiously well informed, but without abstract analysis, practically. Whether they analyse it in these terms or not, most voters just want what they would consider the good judgment of their MP. A well-run constituency office, fine speeches, and a good newsletter are incidentals, not noticed by most voters. A candidate's judgment will generally best be judged by party affiliation.

If it is a virtue of our present way of voting that it practically enables the voters to choose a government, is the representative, the MP, reduced to a mere token or lever to support a government? Should we do better to vote directly for a choice of government? No. The MP's role as the voter's representative remains essential. Only she can hold a government to its principles, scrutinize its conduct, and withdraw her confidence if incompetence or corruption or betrayal of principle indicate. We may be cynical about this happening, but it should at least be possible.

If we elect an MP of the party that forms the government, elect her because that is her party, we still expect her to see that the government does what it said it would do, is honest, and responds to developments consistent with its principles and the good of the country. Should new issues arise that may divide the party, even split it, we expect her to use her judgment in the interest of the country.

We do not in choosing a government in an election set up a party dictatorship. The government is responsible to and at the mercy of the House of Commons. We cannot govern ourselves. I have tried to show that it is a delusion to think that the voters' will on the myriad decisions of government could be extracted by any system of voting. So we choose someone we can trust, influenced most by her commitment to a party, and leave it to her.

Runoff, Etc.

The possibility of members being elected with a third or less of the votes when there are as many parties as there have been in Canada recently encourages thoughts of different ways of electing members, even in single-member ridings and without aiming at proportional representation. How can Jones, the Liberal, represent a riding where he got only 29 per cent of the vote against 27 per cent for the New Democrat, 25 per cent for the Alliance candidate, and 19 per cent for the Progressive Conservative?

The simple answer is that the 71 per cent who did not vote for Jones cannot mind him much if they did not coalesce around one of his opponents. Very likely he was a popular second choice and would have won under one or another alternative election procedure. But every other election procedure runs up against the paradox of voting and can produce questionable results.

A series of ballots, or a preferential ballot in which a series of ballots is anticipated in one cast, runs the risk that an eliminated candidate may be the most popular second choice. I showed above how, with the alternative vote, more votes can lead to a candidate losing.

Another scheme is what is called an exhaustive vote, where no candidates are eliminated but the voting goes on until someone gets a majority – the procedure used to elect a pope. In practice, candidates are dropped or drop out after a poor early showing, and the results and the problems may be the same as with an elimination ballot. Where an exhaustive ballot drags on until it becomes exhausting, a majority vote becomes an accident. On a further ballot there could be a different result.

In Their Dreams

The claims made for electoral reform, beyond the question-begging claim that it is fairer insofar as it produces proportional representation, are, to put it politely, wishful thinking without basis in evidence or reason. Whatever ails us – politicians untrusted, low voter turnout, policies people dislike, partisanship, party discipline – reformers claim that a new electoral system will cure it.

A faint plausibility appears in the claim that partisanship is reduced in multi-party politics. The constant need for coalitions forces some parties to work together in government. But there is no measure of partisanship or basis for verifying the claim. The most extreme political conflict in a democracy is in Taiwan, where a mishmash electoral system gives several parties seats in the Yuan, and violent brawls have broken out several times.

More importantly the smoothing out of conflict, the cooperation and consensus that reformers claim for their dream world, is not evidently a good thing. Politics is about real conflicts of ideas and interests. However empty and dishonest partisan slanging may be, it is the decay of a real and necessary part of politics. Politics where parties regularly in government settle things quietly between themselves, where there is no opposition as we know it, only marginalized parties like the Italian Communists, stifle debate, and accountability.

There is still plenty of partisanship in elections in multi-party systems, but most of what goes on in elections is phoney: claims made for policies that will only be implemented if shared with other parties, or claims for the superiority of this party over that party when both will be cosy together in government after the election.

If parties in multi-party elections get on so well, why do they not merge? Even in the days of mass membership parties, the real party was, as it is now, the members of the party apparatus, the insiders. For them, the party means jobs, influence, and prestige that can be more easily had in an existing party, however small, than fought for in a big party. In Europe, parties are largely state financed, and as long as the money keeps coming the party leadership keeps going.

Indeed, far from reducing partisanship, electoral reform fosters it. It breeds parties. Parties came into being in the House of Commons so that people, ideas, and interests could coalesce and be made to work together. Proportional representation perversely sanctions division. Some parties exist out of pure partisanship. Nothing in ideas, interests, or affinities distinguished Italian Liberals or Republicans from many in the Christian Democratic Party except their adherence to their separate parties.

It Matters

What does it all matter? There are prosperous peaceful countries with proportional representation. The rule of law, freedom, and some kind of democracy strongly correlate with peace and prosperity, but the technicalities of the electoral system?

'It does not much matter' is hardly the basis for a great reform movement. The reformers think it matters, very much. If their arguments are sound and proportional representation or the STV is 'the thing,' as reformers believe, the results of every election in Canada's history have been monstrously wrong and only the enthusiasts for reform have noticed. Surely people should be fighting in the streets over such an injustice and affront to democracy. But there is something unreal about the arguments for electoral reform. If people can be persuaded to tell pollsters that they favour electoral reform, they do not seem to think it very important. Only a tiny number of academics and enthusiasts promote it strenuously.

But it does matter. A country can take a great deal of strain. Canada has struggled to remain united for decades. The Netherlands, Italy, Austria, and Denmark have survived stagnant, confused, and unresponsive politics for decades. Should Canada add to its strains and adopt an electoral system that puts government beyond control of the voters? No.

F.A. Hermens argued persuasively in *Democracy or Anarchy*,[48] first published in 1941, that proportional representation led to dictatorship in Italy and Germany. His argument was widely entertained but later forgotten. Proportional representation's advocates take it as an insult. Plainly, proportional representation in most of Europe has not led to fascism since the war. It probably did facilitate communist takeovers in Eastern Europe. Hermens did not argue that it led ineluctably to dictatorship. His argument was that the division, fostering of extremes, incapacity, and irresponsibility produced by proportional representation made countries under great strain, like Italy after the First World War or Germany in the Depression, vulnerable to dictatorship.

Post-war European politics was heavily circumscribed. Pre-war fascist and authoritarian movements had often been extinguished or were banned. Recovery fuelled by the Marshall Plan and the American alliance in the Cold War took priority over politics. Then a Europe of bureaucratic administration more and more superseded national politics as the source of law and politics and a place to find a career of influence. And Western Europe at peace under American protection and increasingly economically united experienced unprecedented prosperity. Political institutions were never seriously tested.

France is a limited exception. An anti-Gaullist might argue that it was another case of proportional representation leading to dictatorship. Certainly proportional representation led to the crisis of 1958, as no government could deal with the strain of the war in Algeria. But de Gaulle was no dictator and the Fifth Republic is not a dictatorship.

7 Ontario's Quiet Referendum: Electoral Reform in Ontario

In May 2007 Ontario's citizens' assembly predictably produced a proportional representation recommendation but, just to be different, it recommended so-called mixed member proportional voting (MMP), rather like German proportional representation.

Ontario is not a natural home for reform, but the Liberals had promised in 2003 to look at it. Having broken a promise not to raise taxes, they felt bound to keep a seemingly insubstantial promise. They did not want change and there was no public clamour for it. But with the new government doing nothing, the minister responsible, the ambitious Attorney General Michael Bryant, began talking about 'a quiet democratic revolution'[49] and as early as December 2003 foretold the assembly's recommendation.

The assembly was not set up until 2006. Despite an elaborate media campaign organized by the assembly staff, its work was ignored by the general public. Some people thought it was a civics exercise put on by the provincial educational TV channel. But once the process started, the drive to a referendum was unstoppable.

The Set-up

A select committee of the legislature that paved the way for the Ontario Citizens' Assembly expressed concern[50] about the self-selection of citizens predisposed to change in the formation of the British Columbia Citizens' Assembly. But nothing was or could be done about that, and the formation and proceedings of the Ontario Citizens' Assembly were much like those in British Columbia. Despite the select committee's caution, self-selection was the principal basis for membership in the assembly. Invitations went out to 123,489 voters and only 7,033 expressed interest. The invitations offered a chance to make history.[51] You do not make history by leaving well enough alone. The assembly report is a bit circumspect about how that number became the 103 members, but together with drawing lots, more self-selection plainly took place. One member said, 'I feel as though I've won the lottery.'[52]

The research staff (including Heather MacIvor, a keen proponent of proportional representation), guest speakers (David Farrell again), and reading were heavily biased toward change. A presentation by Ivan Fellegi, Canada's chief statistician, outlining the make-up of Ontario's population, had on the face of it nothing to do with electoral reform. But it carried the implication that a good election would produce a pictorial representation of the population – a false understanding of representative democracy common in reformers.

The assembly was overwhelmingly for change, as were those who made submissions to them, proving how unrepresentative they all were. Six hundred and eighty-two submissions advocated change, against only seventy-two submitting that there should be no change. No poll shows 90 per cent support for change. In its deliberation phase the assembly began with the design of new electoral systems for Ontario. Its first vote, on 1 April 2007, was a choice between MMP and STV – won seventy-five votes to twenty-five by MMP. Only two weeks later did the assembly vote on whether to stick with the current system or go for MMP, eighty-six voting for change and surprisingly, after what they had been through, sixteen for the existing system. The next day they voted ninety-four to eight to recommend MMP to the people of Ontario.

The vote to choose between alternative systems of proportional representation before deciding whether change was necessary was typical of the bias of the proceedings. They began with a learning phase in which they were softened up by the description of a cornucopia of alternative electoral systems, with the claims made for them presented uncritically. The existing system was reduced by academic analysis to SMP or single-member plurality voting – a construct without a history and with nothing much to say for itself. During the consultation phase they listened mainly to keeners for reform, long-standing Green Party stalwarts among them. In the deliberation phase they began by designing two proportional representation systems: actually, working out, under academic instruction, the details of how MMP and STV could apply in Ontario. They spent much time in the proportional representation fan's pointless pursuit of mathematical proportionality. They considered the Imperiali, D'hondt, Droop, and Sainte-Laguë formulae for allocating seats before settling on Hare and modelled how the systems might work on the basis of speculations on how we would vote, measuring the results by the Loosemore-Hanby index of proportionality. What was the likelihood that the assembly would say that it had wasted all its time and effort and the present system worked well enough?

In their learning phase the assembly members were told to think of their task as like the choice of a car.[53] They should consider the various features they might want and see which model offered the best mix. Features on offer were suggested by the Principles and Characteristics set out in the Regulation establishing the assembly:

- *Legitimacy*: The electoral system should have the confidence of Ontarians and reflect their values.
- *Fairness of representation*: The Legislative Assembly should reflect the population of Ontario in accordance with demographic representation, proportionality, and representation by population, among other factors.
- *Voter choice*: The electoral system should promote voter choice in terms of quantity and quality of options available to voters.
- *Effective parties*: Political parties should be able to structure public debate, mobilize and engage the electorate, and develop policy alternatives.
- *Stable and effective government*: The electoral system should contribute to continuity of government, and governments should be able to develop and implement their agendas and take decisive action when required.
- *Effective Parliament*: The legislative assembly should include a government and opposition, and should be able to perform its parliamentary functions successfully.
- *Stronger voter participation*: Ontario's electoral system should promote voter participation as well as engagement with the broader democratic process.
- *Accountability*: Ontario voters should be able to identify decision-makers and hold them to account.[54]

People know what a car is for. Do they know what voting is for? They do. Voting is a way of making decisions, in a general election deciding who will govern. But the clever bureaucrats and academics who ran the assembly in their crude abstract analysis failed to grasp the first thing about voting.

It is as if, being shown a car's air conditioning, seating, luggage capacity, and sound system, we thought a car was not for getting from A to B but somewhere to keep cool, to hang out with friends, to store stuff, or to listen to music.

When coming up with homey analogies, the assembly staff would have done better to think of friends out together choosing a restaurant: will it be Thai, Italian, Chinese, or steak? They could make a draw, roll a die, or vote. Voting is a way of deciding. But if the friends took guidance from a citizens' assembly, they could end up with no decision or in negotiations on how to split the meal between a starter at one restaurant, a main course at another, and dessert at a third. Before they had worked it all out, the restaurants would have been closed.

The Principles and Characteristics are vague and seemingly innocuous and uncontroversial, but they gave a vigorous spin to the proceedings. Of course elections should have legitimacy, but who says they don't now? Fans of proportional representation. Fairness of representation invokes the false pictorial idea of representation and slips in proportionality as a given when whether fairness demands it should be an open question. Voter choice implies the elaborate ballots popular with electoral reformers that ask voters to make more choices than they seriously can while giving them no effect. Effective parties are parties that can form a government but the Characteristic misses that basic point. Stable and effective government and effective Parliament attempt to pre-empt the argument that electoral reform leads to unstable and ineffective government by boldly questioning the obvious. Stronger voter participation plays into the groundless claims of electoral reformers that reform will increase turnout. The assembly had the honesty to disclaim any impact on turnout for its proposal. Accountability is obviously necessary and obviously available now, but as with the first Principle it invites the whingeing of reformers, though who would be accountable for electoral reform when it all went wrong and the citizens had disappeared?

How It Wouldn't Work

The assembly's proposal was that 90 members of the provincial parliament be elected in the old-fashioned way in single-member constituencies. A further 39 members would be elected from party lists on the basis of proportional representation. Many voters will think that this is a kind of compromise, not even half proportional representation but 39/129 proportional representation. Proponents of the scheme will be content that they think that. It is not even clear that the assembly understood it correctly as MMP was classed in its deliberations as a 'mixed system.' But the 39 list seats would not be assigned in proportion to party votes. They would be used to see that, as far as mathematically possible, each party would get seats in proportion to its party vote. So a party none of whose candidates won 1 of the 90 constituency seats but that got 10 per cent of the party vote would get 14 seats. A party that got 59 constituency seats with 45 per cent of the vote – easy enough as we are continually reminded by fans of proportional representation – would get none of the 39 list seats. The 39 list seats would not 'introduce an element of proportionality' in the Law Commission's phrase. They would impose proportional representation.

The assembly's triumphant slogan was 'One ballot, two votes,' offering the promise of more choice. But it is a cheat. Each ballot would ask for a vote for a constituency candidate and a vote for a party. The voter who voted for a winning candidate would effectively cancel his second party vote. Only the voter whose constituency vote was in the theory of proportional representation 'wasted' could cast an effective list vote.

The only 'mixed' element in MMP was the retention of single-member constituencies. We were assured that we should still have our local member for a riding, only a bit larger than now. Fewer than half the members would come from party lists and not represent a riding. While so far as it goes the retention of local members is a good thing, even local members under MMP would necessarily be more party creatures, as their local success or failure would rebound on the party list.

The belief that retaining local members while rigorously imposing proportional representation strikes a good balance results from an overly abstract analysis of voting in which our vote is broken down into a vote for a local representative and a vote for a government, a vote for a person and a vote for a party. When we vote now we are not torn, as academics suppose, between these two or any other factors. We weigh them and much more in making a decision. Is Smith for gun control, lower taxes, withdrawal from Afghanistan? Is she a good speaker but an indifferent servant of the constituents, famously accomplished but a stranger to the riding?

We cannot split our votes for each consideration, a vote for someone to speak in the House, a vote for someone to serve the constituents, a vote on this issue and that. It is not only impractical but also wrong because, whatever the considerations of policy and principle, ability and character we may weigh, we are voting for a human being to represent us who will be called upon to do all that a member may do and to address all issues that may arise.

Though independents may be elected in the constituency seats under MMP, most constituency members would be elected for a party, and the party, as now, would be the prime consideration in voters' minds. But supporting a party in an election now means hoping that it will form a government. Under MMP there would be no hope of one party forming a government.

The assembly was torn between fear that the election of thirty-nine members from party lists would give parties too much power and the hope that they would produce a better, more pictorially correct representation of the voters. They spent much time considering how parties could be made to offer the right sort of people. They considered having Elections Ontario regulate the selection of party lists. If, getting hold of the wrong end of the stick, electoral reformers can make electing the legislature complicated and inept, the task of figuring out how a party with perhaps tens of thousands of members should come up with an ordered list of thirty-nine candidates defeated the assembly. That they even contemplated government intrusion into the internal workings of parties, intending a specific correct outcome, is alarming. They settled on simple publication of the lists and details of the process used to create them. Parties, however much they may try, in fact or in appearance, to involve the grass roots, will end up creating lists by politburo. The assembly holds to the hope that parties would make up lists for the sake of appearance with gender, ethnicity, and so on correctly observed. As few voters are likely to make much of the individuals on a long list, they may well be sold as coming from the right categories.

This is rigging the system to elect not the individuals we would vote for if left to our free choice but those based on their categories whom the correct think we should elect. But the rigging would not produce a pretty picture. Assuming parties felt compelled to produce correct lists, the correct individuals would necessarily be doubly tokens, elected only as party counters in the parliamentary game and party creatures owing their seats to the party having chosen them for their gender, or race, or ethnicity, and presumptively unable to win seats for themselves.

Such engineered diversity would vary among parties. The larger parties, winning most of the constituency seats, would see few elected from their lists, however correct. Smaller parties would have caucuses made up all or mostly from their lists.

MMP would produce two classes of MLA. Constituency members would have their constituency duties with the work and hope of local strength that they carry. List members would be free of local duties but indentured party servants.

The assembly settled on a 3 per cent threshold, below which a party would receive no list seats – just enough to exclude the Family Coalition Party, whose candidates received 2.7 per cent of the vote in 1990. Or perhaps not. The Family Coalition Party ran only sixty-eight candidates in the then 130 ridings in Ontario. With MMP they could likely have got over 3 per cent of the party vote with no more effort and four seats. Under MMP small parties can forego local campaigning and pick up list votes and seats with a province-wide campaign giving economies of scale, a kind of bulk buying of votes.

Decoys

Advocates of MMP tout it as offering more choice. As we have seen, this is a con for the voter who votes for X party's candidate in a riding and X party's list. But you can split your vote, the MMP touts proclaim: vote for X party's candidate and Y party's list. Why would you want to do that? Can't make up your mind? If you voted for the X candidate, you must surely want X strong in government. The possibility that it is the X party candidate, despite the X party, that you want in government is an abstract analysis meaningless in concrete reality. If you vote for the X party candidate despite the party, party cannot mean much to you and your party vote cannot mean much to you.

MMP fans think of splitting your vote as being broadminded, not bound to a party. But as proportional representation, which MMP is, is designed entirely to serve parties and entrench them, its advocates cannot pretend to such indifference to party. They are trying to suck and blow.

If you decide to split your vote, the likelihood is that you are onto the MMP con and know your list vote may be wasted. So you vote tactically for the party most likely to ally itself with your real party choice – a risky vote, as post-election alliances can be unpredictable. Ideally you could vote to elect a candidate of one party in your riding and support the list of another party that would agree on everything with your riding candidate's party.

Thus is born the idea of a decoy party. Suppose there is a 200-seat House with 100 seats filled by riding candidates and 100 from party lists. Tories run in the ridings but no Conservatives. With 35 per cent of the vote, the Tories elect 40 members in the ridings. There is no Tory list for the party vote but there is a Conservative list. It gets 35 per cent of the vote and 70 list seats. The Tories/Conservatives have elected 110 members, 55 per cent, with 35 per cent of the vote. Hard to do, even with our present way of voting.

The assembly dismisses the decoy problem in a footnote in its full report.[55] Blatant decoy parties could be banned by legislation. But the possibility of decoy parties shows a fundamental flaw in MMP. The two votes on one ballot are only useful or effective if there is something like a decoy party available. In practice, parties can become effective decoys without planning bold enough to be caught by legislation. In Germany the Free Democrats have operated as a decoy for the Christian Democrats. The differences between them on policy were no greater than differences within the Christian Democrats and the relations between their politicians as cordial or bitter as those among Christian Democrats. In election after election Christian Democrat voters having elected a constituency member have given their list vote to the Free Democrats, accounting for roughly half their votes, often carrying them over the 5 per cent threshold.

In the 1994 German election, for instance, the Christian Democrats[56] elected 221 constituency members with 45 per cent of the vote and the Free Democrats none with 3.3 per cent of the vote. In the list vote, the Christian Democrats fell to 41.4 per cent and the Free Democrats rose to 6.9 per cent – an almost exact transfer of 3.6 per cent of the votes. The Christian Democrats got seventy-three list members and the Free Democrats forty-seven. Overall the governing coalition got 50.7 per cent of the seats with 48.8 per cent of the votes. If there had been no shift of votes, the Christian Democrats would have picked up only eight more seats while the Free Democrats would have got none. Even if there had been no 5 per cent threshold and the Free Democrats had been awarded list seats for 3.3 per cent of the vote, the coalition would have been worse off by about twenty seats and lost its majority. Such shifts partly account for the unusual stability of German politics, despite proportional representation. The Social Democrats in time found their decoy in the Greens.

In the 2009 German election the Christian Democrat list votes were about 2,388,000 fewer than its constituency votes, and the Free Democrat list votes were about 2,238,000 more, gaining them about thirty more seats and assuring a comfortable majority for the anticipated coalition. As usual, the 4,075,115 Free Democrat constituency votes were 'wasted.'

Adventitious decoys like the German Free Democrats can only survive if they do not become blatant or formalized, risking legal challenge. They must be unreliable and ready to cheat those who use them, as the Free Democrats have done. Even without cheating, Christian Democrats have reasonably resented the Free Democrats' disproportionate role in German politics based on Christian Democrat votes.

The decoy problem is peculiar to MMP but typical of the problems that arise with every contrivance to do better than best. Every complication intended to right imagined wrongs produces real wrongs.

Making the sorry best of MMP depends on a thorough grasp of how it works and a knowledge of what one's fellow voters will do that few polls can give. There is every reason to believe that many people will not understand how it works and what they should do. Surveys done in Scotland after MMP was adopted for elections to the Scottish Parliament showed woeful incomprehension. Under the slogan 'Second vote Green' the Scottish Greens played on this, encouraging voters to see the list vote as a second preference, when of course in fact for the overall result the list vote rules.[57]

The Ontario Citizens' Assembly fretted about many details, but the details matter less than they think. Like many reformers, they succumb to the delusion that salvation is in the details. MMP is proportional representation and bad because proportional representation is bad. All that distinguishes it from straight old-fashioned Italian proportional representation is a con.

Sore Losers

The government had promised to hold a referendum if the citizens' assembly recommended a new electoral system. Anticipating the inevitable, the necessary legislation was introduced as the assembly began is work and passed a few weeks before it issued its report.

The referendum was held concurrently with Ontario's first fixed-date election on 10 October 2007. Voters were offered a choice between what was called on the ballot 'first-past-the-post' and MMP. Over 63 per cent voted for the way we do things now and a majority in 102 of the 107 ridings. 'First-past-the-post' met the threshold of 60 per cent of the votes and 50 per cent of the ridings that advocates of MMP objected was unfair to their side. Ninety-seven per cent of those who voted, voted in the referendum.

Well before the vote and without any polls to show how the vote might go, the advocates of proportional representation began a great whinge that the referendum was unfair. The objection that the supermajority required for victory was unfair was undermined by their resounding defeat. In any case, high thresholds for constitutional change are commonplace and wise. It might be otherwise if we were offered a chance to revisit the issue at each election, but we were not. New Zealand voters were assured when they voted 54 per cent for MMP that they would be offered a chance to change their minds. They have not been.

It was also objected that holding the referendum with the election denied it the attention it deserved. It did not seem to matter in British Columbia in 2005 when STV got 57 per cent of the vote in a referendum held with a general election. Rather a separate referendum would be unfair, as it would dragoon opponents of change into coming out to vote against something when they just wanted to be left in peace. The appeal of a separate referendum to proportional representation's proponents is that it would be an opportunity for the enthusiasts to troop out for their pet scheme while the unpersuaded carried on with their lives. As it is, it can be assumed that 99 per cent of the supporters of proportional representation got out to vote for it, while many who did not approve did not find the time to vote.

The Quiet Referendum

The whingers' principal complaint was that their message did not get across. This was partly a repeat of the objection that in an election period it did not get the attention they thought it deserved. But it was a dull election, and if MMP was as appealing as they claimed, it should easily have attracted attention.

The whingers seemed to think it was the government's job to get out the vote for MMP. Elections Ontario spent almost $7 million on an 'education' program, sending out leaflets, running ads in all media, and sending out 'resource officers' to talk down to community groups. A supposedly impartial government body 'educating' the public on a referendum issue is not as wholesome as it may seem. As a thought experiment, think of an election in which the parties and candidates do not campaign but the election commission educates the public on

the platforms and records of the parties and the careers, accomplish-
ments, and characters of the candidates. Done with scrupulous impartiality, this would give unmerited plausibility to the partisan claims of
parties and candidates. But such impartiality is humanly impossible.
Inevitably the bureaucrats' biases would affect their presentation and
· we should be led astray.

When a referendum was held in Ireland in 2001 on the Nice Treaty
changing the institutional structure and proceedings of the European
Union, the government's Referendum Commission ran ads saying
basically that the countries of Europe had met together to agree to
measures for the peace and prosperity of Europe and voters were being
asked to say yes or no to peace and prosperity. The Irish voters had the
gumption to say no. It did not matter, as Europe will not take no for an
answer.

In fact Elections Ontario's education campaign was strongly biased
in favour of MMP. Its account of our present way of voting and MMP
was superficial and inaccurate. It said that under both systems the party with the largest number of seats would be invited to form the government, which is not quite true as it stands and is certainly not true
under proportional representation. Just ask the Christian Democrats,
who had the largest number of seats after the 1969 West German election but were passed over for the Social Democrats. Elections Ontario
referred voters to the citizens' assembly website – pure propaganda for
MMP.[58] There was no balancing website referred to for the merits of the
way we do things now.

The parties were banned from campaigning on the referendum issue.
This did not inhibit New Democrats and Greens, in the pursuit of disproportionate power, from speaking up for MMP. Liberals and PCs
were inhibited from taking a position by the claim of proportional representation's fans that they cling to the status quo out of interest. John
Tory, the PC leader, known to be doubtful, was lambasted by MMPs'
supporters for not getting his name removed from an anti-MMP website.[59] In fact there are plenty of wets on the issue in all parties. Several
prominent Liberals, most notably Michael Bryant, did voice their support for MMP, without being attacked for their intervention. If proportional representation means that a party can never fully win an election
and take responsibility for government it also means that a party never
really looses and the narrow party of insiders is always in and wheeling
and dealing.

The MMP forces were able to claim all party support with Ed Broadbent, Hugh Segal, and Carolyn Bennett, certified members of the chattering classes' the great and the good, patrons of their campaign. MMP had a running start with electoral reform lobbies like Fair Vote Canada ready to morph into registered referendum campaigns. Only one small group was able to organise in opposition with a quixotic offshoot in Nipissing. Various labour and left-wing groups organised to campaign for MMP. The MMP side had eight registered campaigns against their opponents' two and outspent them fifty to one.

Reported comments of voters and the *Globe and Mail*'s editorial position[60] showed many were dissatisfied with first-past-the-post but not persuaded that MMP was the answer. But the proponents of any reform scheme deserve defeat partly on the resistance of those who think there could be a better scheme. Once people fancy that some contrivance and complication would be better than what is tried and true, a multitude of options and quibbles pop up, and none will be satisfied.

The problem the enthusiasts for proportional representation faced was that in their blinkered perspective its merits were obvious and all that needed to be done was say what it was and voters would support it overwhelmingly. They were reduced to resentful arguments that their opponents were corrupt and fear mongering. But as usual they had it backwards. Proportional representation only triumphs when the political factions have an interest in it, and its strongest support came from the New Democrat and Green interests. Four of the five ridings that backed MMP were NDP strongholds. The idea is simple enough. Voters got it and did not like it.

As the opponents of MMP began to make their case, they were immediately denounced by Vote for MMP:

> Old guard politicians, and their hangers-on and the sponsors behind them, especially the private media owners ...
>
> The old guard, its excessive power imperiled, is now spreading black propaganda, misinformation and confusion about MMP ...
>
> Hysteria and dirty tricks will increase as MMP gets closer to victory ... It may resort to negative TV ads.[61]

Sadly, No to MMP did not have the money for TV ads, but happily MMP never got close to victory. The *Toronto Star*, of all papers, was accused of being anti-Italian for referring to the sorry history of proportional representation in Italy.[62]

The rather Maoist tone of these attacks was consistent with the contention of Vote for MMP that it was the role of the government to educate voters to vote correctly.

Vote for MMP showed itself particularly sensitive on the issue of how party lists would be chosen, calling it a 'big lie' that the candidates on the list would be appointed by the parties. All parties were pressed to assure that the lists would be drawn up democratically, but, as the citizen's assembly recognized in not attempting to tell parties how they should make up lists, whatever the democratic show, thousands of party members cannot put together an ordered list of thirty-nine candidates. They can only endorse what the leadership devises.

After the referendum, two academics purported to demonstrate,[63] using opinion surveys in which Ontarians were asked select and loaded questions, that the result would have been the reverse of what it was if 'all citizens had known':

1. that MMP would give voters two votes, elect some members whose names never appear on a ballot, produce proportional outcomes with more parties and infrequent majorities; and
2. that Assembly members 'were ordinary Ontarians,' 'had an equal chance of being chosen,' 'represented all parts of Ontario,' 'became experts on electoral systems,' and 'most members wanted what's best for all Ontarians' (rather than themselves).

They could not have known all that, as it is not all true. More importantly it is not the whole truth. What the survey showed was simply that people who could give a partial capsule summary of how MMP is supposed to work and had followed and bought into the citizens' assembly were likely to support MMP. Of course they would, because such people were the keeners for electoral reform.

Vote for MMP relied heavily on the citizens' assembly process in its propaganda. It was always their tool, and they expected it to con the voters into thinking that they had already decided in favour of MMP.

The different result in British Columbia in 2005 is explained partly by its different political culture but principally by the backing of the political establishment. The NDP is stronger than in Ontario and keen on reform. The Liberals, a resurrected party, twice shut out of the legislature in the eighties, sold themselves as the party of democratic reform. Though the citizens' assembly show was put on and propaganda was largely left to the assembly, the parties were onside. The ups and downs of British Columbia's politics encourage its politicians to back a system that assures them of some permanent place. Six parties had members in the legislature in the last thirty years, and three won at least two elections but were also wiped out or almost wiped out.

For MMP supporters, it was the big issue. Ontarians, as the government's website had it, were making their 'big decision.' The little interest that MMP attracted comes as a big disappointment. But what could they expect? If all opposition is cowed into silence or denounced as corrupt and voters are simply to be educated to make the correct choice, what excitement can there be?

It Haunts Us Still

Four years after British Columbia voters came close to approving STV, it was decisively rejected in a second referendum. Over 60 per cent voted to stick with our old ways. What had changed?

The 2005 votes came close on the heels of the citizens' assembly proceedings and report with its propaganda and largely soft coverage fresh in voters' minds. The 1996 and 2001 elections had produced unusual results: an NDP majority based on fewer votes than the Liberals in 1996 and a Liberal landslide of seventy-seven of seventy-nine seats on 57.6 per cent of the vote in 2001. In the 2005 election the NDP won thirty-three seats with 41 per cent of the vote, and they seemed for a time likely to win in 2009. Many New Democrats became sceptical of STV. The ballot was changed from a simple yes or no to a choice between FPTP and STV. Voters were provided with details of the twenty ridings, with from two to seven seats proposed for STV. A million dollars of public money was split between STV and No STV campaigns, though STV still had greater resources. The No STV voices were heard. In calm, without the citizens' assembly con, the British Columbia voters gave their final answer.

Voters in Prince Edward Island rejected MMP by 64 per cent on 25 November 2005. Interest has faded in Quebec and New Brunswick. But developments in the United Kingdom may revive interest.[64] Fair Vote Canada and other lobbies and enthusiasts will not shut up. We must be armed against a resurgence of electoral follies.

8 Parliamentary Reform

Free at Last

In a celebrated incident in April 1998, Liberal MP Carolyn Bennett wept as she voted with the government for limited compensation for Canadians who may have contracted hepatitis C from tainted blood. This was held up as the most poignant example of an MP forced to vote as her party directs. If she had been free to vote as she wished, she would have voted for unlimited compensation. Her tears were thought to express her frustration at being forced to vote with the government, as much as her sympathy for those denied compensation.

What forced her to vote with the government? Is it set down in an act of Parliament that MPs must vote as their party directs? No. Is it a rule of the House of Commons? No. Is there even a rule of the Liberal Party? No.

What would have happened to her if she had voted against the government? Perhaps she would have been denied a committee appointment she coveted. Perhaps her chances of getting into the Cabinet would have been reduced. As it was, she had to wait until Paul Martin became prime minister to enter the Cabinet. Perhaps she would have been expelled from the Liberal Caucus. So what? She would still have had her seat, her office, and her salary. In time, before the next election, she would likely have been welcomed back among her Liberal pals. What of all these consequences anyway? Conviction should be made of sterner stuff than to be swayed by such considerations.

And what would be wrong with such consequences? Would they be punishment for indiscipline? Why should a government that judged they were doing all they properly could, not shun someone who spurned their judgment, perhaps, as it might seem to them, from emotion or vanity? Bennett was a Liberal. She ran as a Liberal and was elected as a Liberal. To do that creditably she must have thought Liberals were well-meaning and sensible people, united by sound principles, in whom she could have confidence and who could have confidence in her. She was entitled to her opinions and the free, if politic, expression of them. When it came to acting, to voting, the meaning of her being a Liberal must have been that the Liberal government was the best government on offer and deserved to be supported.

Some people may run as Liberals because they calculate that that is the surest way to get elected, with no regard for Liberal people or principles. Entering Parliament so cynically, they are in no position to stand on principles. Surely Dr Bennett could not be one of those. She must simply have become confused. Her confusion is at the base of all calls for free votes, a slackening of party discipline, and parliamentary reform.

The phrase *party discipline* is misleading. It suggests MPs lined up like pupils in a school of early in the last century, kept in order by a strap-wielding teacher, or soldiers in a platoon terrorized by their sergeant. However trite, a better analogy is a team. MPs must indeed be team players. The whips are their captains. They must not put scoring points themselves ahead of the team winning.

If Carolyn Bennett had voted against the government all on her own, with such consequences for herself as we have described, it would have made no difference. The Liberals had a comfortable majority. The bill would have passed. If enough other Liberal MPs had joined her, the bill would have been defeated. As it involved spending money, about a billion dollars in fact, it was undoubtedly a matter of confidence and the government would have fallen. As no one else could have formed a government in that House of Commons, an election would have followed with much confusion about where the rebel Liberals stood. Having broken with their party on an issue of confidence, could they be counted on to support another Liberal government?

It is in this consequence of defeat, the fall of the government, that the issue of free votes is widely understood. On matters of any importance, government MPs must vote with the government or it will fall. Opposition parties often promote a more extreme proposition, that any defeat of a government motion must lead to the government's fall. The Reform Party, which had cultivated a reputation for fiscal restraint, was blithely prepared to vote for an extra billion of spending in order to defeat, or at least embarrass, the government.

Why, ask the advocates of free votes, must the government fall if it is defeated? Because government is not a series of isolated measures. Another billion does not come from nowhere. Either the debt would be that much higher, or other spending would be cut or taxes raised. It is the business of government to weigh all considerations and act coherently. The government had decided that limited compensation was the best it could do, and that judgment could not be rejected without rejecting the whole government of which that judgment was an integral part. A free vote, in the sense of a vote on which the government would not stand or fall, on such an issue, would be an irresponsible vote, in which MPs would try to take credit for a bounty without responsibility for the debt, taxes, or spending cuts that it must entail.

Carolyn Bennett, had she been dictator, could perhaps have found the extra billion to her satisfaction. But the decision was not hers. It was Parliament's. In voting she had to consider what was the best that Parliament at that time could do. Evidently, for her, that was what the Liberal government would do. She had to cast her vote in the real world in which there are only a limited number of possible governments. A Reform/Bloc coalition supported by renegade Liberals would have given her the extra billion but with God knows what confusion and, for her, horrors besides. What is meant by a free vote is really an irresponsible vote by which the individual MP can seek credit for a popular stand without bearing responsibility for the consequences across government.

Typical free votes in the House of Commons have been on issues like abortion or capital punishment, which are supposed to touch politicians' generally obscure consciences. Against these it is supposed no party discipline can or should be imposed. More importantly, these issues can be isolated from the rest of government action. Their financial implications are not material. The social consequences of abortion policy may in the long term be profound. In the near term it makes little difference to what governments do, whether abortion is restricted or not. Such free votes have in any event been just for show. No free vote has ever frustrated the wishes of the government.

Paul Martin's partly free vote over gay marriage illustrated this point. With the Cabinet ranged to vote for it, the result was never really in doubt, and the government was ready to claim credit for the result. Stephen Harper's free vote over reversing that result was another kind of show. He had not promised to end gay marriage, only to have a free vote on it – a free vote he knew would be defeated, even if he won a majority. Martin held a free vote but claimed credit for the government. Harper held a free vote but used its defeat to reassure fearful progressives.

The mass of legislation passed by Parliament from year to year is, rightly or wrongly, uncontroversial. Much is passed with support from some or all opposition parties. Legislation is introduced after wide consultation, to which MPs who have any thoughts may contribute, with further opportunities for discussion in the privacy of caucus, so stray votes against it would hardly be noticed. So they do not occur.

Governments can be defeated on significant legislation and survive. It happens regularly at Westminster. The Iron Lady saw scores of government defeats in her eleven years as prime minister. Tony Blair's government was defeated in November 2005 over the Terrorism Bill and in January 2006 over amendments to the Racial and Religious Hatred Bill, and his government carried on, regardless.

What is a matter of confidence, what must be passed or the government cannot carry on, is a matter of practical judgment. Is the measure central to government policy, something it ran on in the last election, or would want to feature in its record in the next election? How does it relate to the rest of what the government is doing? Will it be unable to do what it wants to do without the legislative tools it is proposing? Any financial measure must fit in with a budget, and that is why financial measures are always matters of confidence.

It may not be the matter itself but the context that makes a vote a matter of confidence. A series of defeats on matters minor in themselves may show that the House is no longer prepared to accept the leadership of the government or that the government has lost touch with its supporters.

Whether another government could be formed from the existing House or an election would likely return a House ready strongly to support the present government or another government must also be taken into account. Confidence can be relative. There must always be a government, and none can have universal, uncritical, unqualified support. Is the government the strongest we can hope for, or could there be a stronger, in the existing House, or after an election?

A minority government obviously cannot get many things it would like passed. So it holds them back. The Harper government has shown a readiness to accept defeat on important measures. It seeks credit from its supporters for trying, while its acceptance of defeat comforts those who fear it. There has been no question of free votes, except on gay marriage. Conservative MPs have been perfectly disciplined. In the context such defeats do not throw into question the qualified confidence a minority government must rely on. It can still get important measures passed with the support or abstention of some opposition parties. There has been no strong likelihood that an election would produce a more effective government.

There are practically no examples of government measures being defeated under majority governments in modern Canada. This is not because the rules prevent it. It is because the MPs, who whinge that they are not free and must tow the party line, will not make it happen.

In February 2001 the Alliance presented a motion requiring the ethics counsellor to report to Parliament rather than to the prime minister, as had been promised by the Liberal Red Book in the 1993 election campaign. The Liberal whips told Liberal members that the government would treat the issue as a matter of confidence and they must vote against it. All but two Liberal MPs did as they were told. Paul Steckle was of one of the several unremarked social conservatives in the Liberal caucus with no prospect of advancement, but Ivan Grose was later made a parliamentary secretary, his advancement unaffected by his rebellion.

The matter was clearly not one of confidence. The government's position could not even be called a bluff. Did Liberal MPs really believe that Chrétien would have called an election if the Alliance motion had passed, going to the voters to campaign against a measure that he had promised to adopt eight years before, a measure that voters must have thought obviously sound or too unimportant to be troubling them with?

In their squawking over parliamentary reform the Alliance proposed there should be 'greater clarity' on what is a matter of confidence. There can be no greater clarity. It is clear enough, but it is a matter of judgment. No rule can govern it. A matter is not one of confidence just because whips say it is.

Nor is it for the opposition to say. During the Pearson minority government the opposition played a game of trying to catch the Liberals out, occasionally pulling off a vote against them and loudly demanding that the government resign. Everyone knew that there was no issue of confidence. Pearson had a quite comfortable minority, able to get support from the New Democrats or Social Credit for practically anything he was inclined to do. But the opposition game-playing encouraged the mistaken notion that the government must win every vote or fall.

Why are government measures not defeated in Canada? There

are several possible reasons. With the work of government divided between Ottawa and the provinces, the volume of legislation passed at each level is less than that at Westminster. The House of Commons in Ottawa is less than half the size of that at Westminster. It is easier for the government to anticipate, accommodate, or forestall political strays. Very few MPs actually have any independent thoughts about what governments do. Among Liberals –and now, evidently, Conservatives – there has been little thought of anything but how to get and hold onto power.

Government measures being defeated may seem a cheering spectacle, and it shows that party discipline is not as brutally strict as MPs pretend, but it shows that something has gone amiss. The government has misjudged what its members will support. One-on-one and in caucus a government must constantly seek assurance that its members are all onside. Whatever MPs say or the press reports, it cannot simply do as it pleases and expect to whip its members into line. It must forego measures that an important number of its members might revolt against.

We do not see this happening, for several reasons. Governments have a constant eye to what will be popular and get them re-elected. So do MPs. What appears politic or impolitic to governments in that perspective will likely appear so to its MPs. When a government idea is opposed by its MPs, it will not be pressed, and the caucus opposition that stopped it will not become public. Even without consulting its MPs, a shrewd government will have a good sense of what they will like and what they will not like. Their influence can be effective without a word spoken. If MPs do have independent thoughts, they will likely be on smaller issues. A backbench MP is in no position to develop an alternative budget or legislative program. If he is not in agreement with the broad direction of government policy, he is in the wrong party.

All votes in Parliament are already free votes, but they are votes with consequences – consequences MPs are often loath to face. Advocates of reform mean something else by 'free votes.' They mean that measures should be brought before Parliament that the government, and perhaps the leaders of the opposition parties, practically take no position on. In the reform optic, to call a vote a free vote is to say that the government either does not care about the issue or does not know what to do about it. A government that does not care about or cannot come to a judgment about important issues is incapable of governing. A practice of allowing free votes would amount to a government having no confidence in itself.

Most talk about free votes has been about government members voting against government measures. On the opposition side, strays have been confined to free votes: Tories supporting gay marriage, a New Democrat opposing it. If government MPs are supposed to back the government 'right or wrong,' opposition MPs are happy to vote on the basis that the government is always wrong, without any strays. If there were a real movement away from straight party voting, for most government strays there would be corresponding opposition strays in the other direction and the same measures would be passed on slightly different votes.

It is government MPs who feel restless under the whip because they are responsible for a government's survival. The freedom they hanker after is the irresponsibility of opposition where members can vote *en bloc* against whatever the government may be doing, even when it is obviously good, on the grounds that it is not enough.

Governments have more means of keeping their members in line, but opposition parties show if anything greater discipline. Why? Because in the end the squawk of members for more freedom is pure self-interest. In opposition the struggle to get into government for the choicer pickings there dominates, and opposition MPs keep ranks to oppose together. Once in government, a few disappointed members want to strike out on their own. As their hopes of a Cabinet seat fade, they look for other ways to make a name for themselves.

Because parties must mean something, they must be able to take a stand together and stick to it. If they cannot, what is the voter to make of parties? Suppose you like the long gun registry and your Tory MP broke with the government to vote against scrapping it. Should you vote for him knowing that his re-election might assure another Tory government opposed to a the long gun registry? Or should you vote against him, even though he is a fine fellow and you agree with his stand? If the party label does not warrant that the candidate generally will take the party line, what does it mean and how can we know what he may stand for?

In the history of the Reform Party, the passage of the Goods and Services Tax (GST) was seen as a classic example of the evils of unfree voting. As Reform saw it, party discipline forced twenty-two of the twenty-three Tory MPs from Alberta to vote for the GST. But nothing forced them. One, David Kilgour, voted against it and spent a pleasant couple of years as an independent MP before being re-elected, the only Alberta MP who was re-elected, this time as a Liberal, and serving nine years in Chrétien's Cabinet. The Tory MPs who voted for the GST actually believed it was a good thing, either after careful thought, or from their respect for Michael Wilson or Don Mazankowski. If Alberta Tory MPs had really believed the GST was a bad thing, what would have kept them from breaking ranks and voting against it? The instinct for political survival would surely have moved some of them to take Kilgour's happy course.

Reform, in any event, was an ambiguous advocate of freedom for MPs. They wanted MPs to be free to vote as their constituents wanted them to. For MPs' alleged slavery to party they would have substituted slavery to the voters. However, what the voters want is often obscure. MPs may be happy to present their claim for more freedom as keenness to do what the people want, to make up a fancied democratic deficit. But the claim does not bear scrutiny.

MPs sometimes claim to have consulted their constituents and voted as they wished. But what the constituents wished is not formally or scientifically determined, may be – not just practically but in principle – impossible to establish. And is the MP who makes such a claim actually deferring to the voters against her better judgment? Or is she one of those politicians uninterested in or incapable of judging what is best and only interested in a popular stand that will get her re-elected?

The late Chuck Cadman kept us in suspense to the last moment as to whether he would vote for or against the Martin government's budget in May 2005. An Independent MP, originally elected for Reform, and espousing its notions of an MP's role, he said he would do what his constituents wanted. It was a fair bet they wanted an election later rather than sooner. That is what voters generally want. But Cadman never proved that that was what his constituents wanted. He simply stood up and voted to keep the Martin government in power. Personal and perhaps public considerations could have induced him to do so. We shall never know. If it had really been his constituents' wishes that decided him, survey results would have told us what they wanted and we should not have been in suspense.

It is odd that, with a generally low opinion of politicians, the public can seem to want to give more power to MPs. It helps to sell the idea that MPs say that they want to oblige the people. But what can an MP do? He has only one vote. It takes another 154 to pass a bill. Such votes are most likely to be found in the MP's own party, where ideology and interest and, perhaps, regard are shared. If a government MP has a good idea, it is best proffered to the responsible minister, and as the parliamentary agenda permits it can be fitted in. If government MPs often had good ideas, this would happen regularly. But there would be something lacking. The MP might be noticed as sound and thoughtful and might one day make it into the Cabinet. But there would be no credit, no fame. If there was credit, it would be the government's. Much better, thinks the MP, to be able to introduce the bill oneself and see it become law.

Let 308 Flowers Bloom

The push for parliamentary reform comes from MPs themselves – those men and women who lack the character and intelligence to make much of the great privilege they gain in being elected. They say they want to do lovely things for the voters. They say they want a role in government. Can they do anything, lovely or not, on their own? What should be their role in government?

Much of the push for parliamentary reform seeks, wittingly or not, to confound the distinction between Parliament and government. In its origin, Parliament had nothing to do with government. Government was in the hands of the King and his servants. Parliament was called to grant money and present grievances. Over the centuries, as governments came to be drawn from and dependent on the support of Parliament, the relation between government and Parliament became intimate. But their roles remained distinct. Eighteenth-century theorists and the authors of the United States Constitution in severing the executive and legislative branches misconstrued this distinction, but it is fundamental. Governments are drawn from Parliament and must have its support, but Parliament does not govern, cannot. The leadership, coherence, and work necessary for government are beyond the capacity of an assembly of hundreds. The role of Parliament, the House of Commons in particular, remains support and scrutiny. It can make or break a government. It should expose and see rectified its failings in detail. But it cannot develop the policies, choose the people, administer the programs, and do all the other work of which government consists.

Historically MPs did not do a lot. Being an MP was a part-time job, if it could be described as a job at all. Parliament sat for perhaps only a few weeks a year. Many MPs seldom spoke. They went to Parliament to keep an eye on the government. They did not expect to do anything much, certainly not to govern, themselves. They brought their judgment and expressed it in voting. They were not so craven before party whips. But that was not because the rules were different. They often had a standing in their communities that gave them independence. They were MPs because they were men of influence. They did not seek to become MPs to become men of influence. MPs are not without influence as Parliament works now. But their influence is rarely seen. MPs want to be seen to be important. To this end, many foolish proposals are advanced.

Reformers want MPs to be able to amend legislation in committees, free of government direction. It is not seriously argued that this would make legislation better. It would simply make MPs feel more important. It is complained that by the time legislation reaches MPs it has had input from and been worked over by bureaucrats, interest groups and their lobbyists, ministers and their aides, and provincial governments. And so it has. And so it should have. It may still be bad legislation. That is a matter of the balance of political forces in the country and received political thought.

Reading the complaints of MPs, one gets the impression that their ideal legislative process would be a kind of group brainstorming in which each MP would get to offer a legislative wish list that would be hashed out through marathon discussion and voting. It would be beyond fantasy to see this happening in the whole House with 308 members, so it is imagined happening in committees. Whatever might issue from the several committees would likely be incoherent and the whole House would still have to flounder about trying to put some order into it.

Legislating, administering, taxing, and spending governments must try to act coherently. They may not do it well. The free-for-all, everyone-does-his-bit model promoted so that MPs can feel better about themselves could never do it at all. It would be a case of too many cooks and no chef. Talk of everyone making a contribution sounds sweet, but nothing gets done without leadership.

The promotion of the MP's role involves rosy talk about what honest and decent people they are, and what experience they bring, and a suggestion of what good work they would do if only they were allowed. They might all be saintly geniuses, but they could not work effectively as is proposed. In fact, they are no better than they should be. These are the MPs who are kept in line by threats of exclusion from committee junkets. Front-bench politicians all incur some odium from their prominence. Backbench politicians escape without notice.

It is complained that by the time it reaches them, legislation has already been carefully drafted. MPs call for matters to come before them in the form of discussion papers or for committees to be able to inquire into issues from scratch, doing without government or royal commission studies. No one should complain that governments inquire deeply, consult widely, confer across departments, and draft bills carefully, except that MPs are left feeling they have nothing to do.

Our MPs have only a small staff, mostly concerned with serving constituents. MPs striving to act independently would indicate that, like the American congressmen they envy, they would each have a large staff trying to keep on top of every issue and interest. Congressmen have scores of staffers. Each congressman tries to be a mini-government independently proposing measures and haggling over or attacking the measures sponsored by other congressmen. Each congressman's mini-government becomes the focus of the flattering attentions of lobbyists.

A foretaste of what MPs want was given by the Commons Agriculture Committee in 2005. In June, with hardly anyone paying attention, the committee, empowered by Paul Martin's appeasement of the parliamentary reform lobby, unanimously added this amendment to a bill before it: 'No person shall market an agricultural product that has a dairy term on the label if the agricultural product is intended as a substitute for a dairy product.'

The intent may have been good or bad.[65] The drafting was bad. It would ban products with recipes on the package saying 'add milk' or 'add butter.' The committee members no doubt thought is was great fun to legislate all on their own without government direction. But the committee acted in ignorance of the conflicting interests affected, without understanding the implications of the language it adopted, and possibly with a push from the dairy lobby – none of which would have happened if the government had not dropped its whip in the hope of making MPs feel better. In October a senior bureaucrat had to explain to the committee what it had done.[66] The legislation, otherwise uncontroversial and worthy, died at the dissolution of Parliament.

MPs' Secrets

In November 2002 Jean Chrétien suffered a defeat on a bizarre procedural reform. In practice the government had decided who would chair the committees of the House of Commons. The Alliance came up with the idea that committees should elect their chairs by secret ballot. With the support of the egregious Carolyn Parrish, then still a Liberal MP, the proposal passed the House Procedure Committee and in the full House passed with the support of fifty-six Liberal MPs, including Paul Martin, then out of office. Fifty-six Liberal MPs bravely defied their oppressive party so that they could timidly vote in secret. Parrish received her reward when she was secretly voted vice-chair of the House Procedure Committee. At one point it was proposed that there be a secret ballot on whether to vote by secret ballot.

The measure is plainly bad and only illustrates the confusion that results when MPs become excited by dreams of power. Who chairs the committees may not much matter, in which case the government choosing them is no tyranny, and conversely MPs should have no fear in publicly rejecting the government's choice. If it is important who chairs the committees, MPs should not be able to do it in secret. We should know who they are voting for and be able to hold them to account for their choices. In fact the committee chairs have serious responsibility for carrying legislation forward. Acceptance of this fact led to a consensus that most committees should be chaired by government members.

In the event Stephen Harper, who had stridently supported the measure, finessed it by arranging that only one Conservative MP of his choosing should be nominated and acclaimed to chair each committee. Such a gambit had been anticipated in the debate over the secret ballot.

Committee Sports

Under the Harper minority government, the House of Commons committees, in which the opposition parties necessarily have a majority, have become a field for political games. Not because individual members have acted on their own but because the opposition parties cooperated in a kind of dry run for the Dion coalition, government measures have been held up and opposition measures have been promoted that the opposition knew it could not pass in the full House without bringing down the government and triggering an election for which they were not ready. The Prime Minister's Office issued a manual to Conservative committee chairs instructing them on tricks to use to thwart opposition ploys. The experience only demonstrates that the idea of committees acting on their own initiative rather than as servants of the House and the government that commands its confidence is unworkable and an opening for politics as sport.

Parliamentary Dithering

Paul Martin pledged himself most loudly to parliamentary reform. It sorted well with his campaign to win the support of Liberal MPs weary of Jean Chrétien and disappointed with the rewards of being government MPs. He made proposals for parliamentary reform in October 2002 when he was out of office and beginning his public campaign to succeed Chrétien. He proclaimed it his first order of business on the day he was sworn in. With much self-congratulation, and quotations from Aristotle and Toqueville, an Action Plan for Democratic Reform[67] was tabled in the House of Commons on 4 February 2004, two days after Martin met Parliament for the first time as prime minister.

The centrepiece of the plan was the introduction, ostensibly modelled on British practice,[68] of one-, two-, and three-line whips. As the Action Plan explained,

- On *one-line free votes*, all government MPs, including Ministers, will be free to vote as they see fit.
- *Two-line free votes* are votes on which the government will take a position and recommend a preferred outcome to its caucus. Ministers are bound to support the government's position on a Two-line vote, as are Parliamentary Secretaries of Ministers affected by it, but other Members are free to vote as they wish.
- A *Three-line vote* will be for votes of confidence and for a limited number of matters of fundamental importance to the government. Government Members will be expected to support the government.
- Most votes will be either two-line or one-line free votes, and Ministers will be unable to take approval for granted. Achieving parliamentary consent will be an exercise in coalition building, and Ministers must earn the support of Members through hard work and active engagement.[69]

Experience under the Martin government says little about how this would work in practice. One-line whips might seem just the thing for Mr Dithers's government. He did too little for us to be sure. The vote on gay marriage was on a two-line whip but always sure of passing and finally claimed as the central achievement of the Martin government. By 2005 the government was so concerned to avoid defeat it was practically extending the whip to opposition MPs.

In practice the three types of whip need make little difference. On most issues, government members would be content to support government measures, regardless of the number of lines on a whip. Behind-the-scenes persuasion would keep possible strays in the fold, much as behind-the-scenes dissidence keeps governments from pressing measures their members do not like. Sure of support, governments would proudly keep down the number of lines on whips as a sign of their benevolence and respect for MPs, knowing they risked nothing thereby.

The Action Plan went on, 'The government will invite all parties to join in this initiative so that all Members of Parliament can represent the views of Canadians and to allow for parliamentary coalitions to be built that cross party lines.'[70] Of course nothing came of that. With or without whips, the opposition parties can be sure their members will oppose.

Other measures, including early referral of legislation to committees, more money for committees, and assurances that they would play a larger role could only be soft soap. The government would condescend to let MPs poke about in the margins of legislation to make them feel better about themselves. But a genuine free-for-all will not work and will not be allowed. In the end, most MPs know that. Dairy labelling before the Agriculture Committee proved it.

Freedom in a Cage

Oddly, some people who want MPs to be free to vote free of the party line do not want MPs to be free to change parties. The defections of Scott Brison and Belinda Stronach to the Liberals, and David Emerson and Whalid Khan to the Conservatives have encouraged a demand that MPs not be allowed to cross the floor or change parties. Members may jump parties for motives that vary from pure and noble to venal. So it is with all political activity. Where there is fault, it may be as much with the party that receives them as in the member who jumps. But it is an essential part of a member's independence that she should be free to change parties. It makes no sense to maintain that members should be free to vote as they like but must sit with and bear the label of the party under whose label they were elected.

Would it have made sense for Belinda Stronach to vote to keep the Liberals in power in June of 2005 but stay with the Tories? Should Stephen Harper have included David Emerson in his Cabinet as a Liberal, making it a mini-coalition? Of course both Stronach and Emerson jumped for a Cabinet seat, giving their moves a taint of corruption. And taking a Cabinet seat amounted to saying that the lot they were days before saying were a menace to the country were all splendid people.

But hard cases make bad law. The Brison, Stronach, Emerson, and Khan jumps were indeed contemptible, as were their receptions by the Liberals and the Conservatives. But politicians could do no good and could not be held responsible if their moves were subject to rules that would restrict them from changing parties. Given what we know about their characters and what they were thinking, would it have been better had they been trapped in the parties for which they were elected by legislation?

A common remedy for the imagined wrong of MPs' freedom to change parties is a requirement that they stand for re-election. Sadly, the Brison and Stronach cases indicate that that would be no remedy. Their re-election does not make what they did any more excusable. It is depressing evidence of the low standards of the voters on whose behalf reformers make such high claims. In any event, a by-election triggered by a member changing parties would be very unsatisfactory. Either the opposition would not be in position to organize, or all the resources of all the contrary parties would be mobilized to defeat the member who had changed parties, rather than voters simply being asked, as they usually are, and should be, whom they want as their MP.

Holding a by-election when a member changes parties is a confused idea. Is it supposed to be a penalty for a wrong? Why should the taxpayers have to pay the costs of such an election? Is it subjecting the member to the will of the voters? It is all right to change parties if the voters approve? From there it is a small step to saying that a member should have to switch parties if the voters' party preferences change.

In any event, a rule against changing parties would preclude one of those many things that are a remote possibility but an essential aspect of politics: political realignment. Parties serve the purpose of bringing people together who can vote together to support a government. Principles, interests, and personal regard coalesce. But principles shift as issues change, interests subside and grow up, personalities fall out and find new regard. Parties must be able to split, merge, disappear, and emerge to seek the coherence that makes government possible. If, when this was happening, all MPs who might be moving were subject to re-election, political development would be inhibited and MPs would be trapped in parties that no longer served their purpose.

There is a recent example. In September 2001 twelve MPs who had left the Alliance caucus, frustrated by Stockwell Day's leadership, formed the Democratic Representative Caucus and went into coalition with the Progressive Conservatives. They were forming a Democratic Representative Association, in effect a new party, but also an affiliate of the Progressive Conservatives, when Day was replaced by Stephen Harper as leader of the Alliance. All is now forgiven and Chuck Strahl of the DRC sits in Stephen Harper's Cabinet with Stockwell Day.

The members of the DRC did not simply jump from one party to another, and their motives were generally judged to be higher than those of Stronach and Emerson, but a rule against changing parties cannot be based on a narrow definition of parties or scrutiny of a member's motives. Why should it not apply to a member who becomes an independent, perhaps expelled from his caucus, or an independent who joins a party?

No one seemed much disturbed by Garth Turner's move from the Conservatives to the Liberals (after a brief flirtation with the Greens) and surely not because he is judged a flibbertigibbet. That he was expelled from the Conservative Caucus, on good grounds, makes no difference. Any MP minded to cross the floor could easily arrange an expulsion.

Another member expelled from his caucus, one-time Liberal Blair Wilson, who had had trouble with his election finances, became the first, and perhaps only, Green MP shortly before the 2008 election. The propriety of his defection received no comment in the excitement of the Greens and the controversy over whether having one MP should entitle the party's leader to a place in the leaders' debates.

To say that MPs should not be allowed to cross the floor could entail that they not be allowed to get themselves expelled from their caucus. If the by-election sanction applied, it would give party caucuses the power to unseat members. MPs would be chained to their parties.

It may be the right thing to change parties. An issue may arise, not live at the time of the election, on which a member differs from his party and agrees with an opposing party. The issues that united him with his party and repelled him from the other may be dead or less pressing. No one can have a mind and be in perfect agreement with his party. A member may honestly and on principle change parties. It was not so in the recent cases. But no rule could govern changes of parties and no judge, still less a Commons committee, could safely judge the sincerity and worthiness of a conversion. The voters will judge the member and the receiving party in due course.

Dictator? What Dictator?

It has become a commonplace to condemn our politics as an elective dictatorship. Once sworn in, the prime minister or the premier can do as he pleases. This is to confuse political ascendancy with institutional power. A prime minister can do nothing without the support of members of Parliament. For some periods this support will be wholehearted and unquestioning – perhaps wrongly, but not because of any fault in our institutions.

Jean Chrétien faced a fractured opposition and led a party interested only in power. He could win election after election and no one would stand up to him because winning elections was all they stood for. Finally, Paul Martin decided he wanted his turn. There was no principle on which he could stand against Chrétien but he seemed to stand for the future of power, and finally Chrétien had to give way and in his last year he was losing his grip on power.

Tony Blair seemed in his early years to be able to have his way on everything. He was even pushing the Queen around. In the end he clung to office but his power ebbed away. He had to yield his place to Gordon Brown. Brown's ascendancy lasted only months. There was a serious prospect that he would be removed before he would face defeat in an election.

Stephen Harper, despite his Reform background, seems to have an even firmer grip on the government than his predecessors. He has achieved a remarkable political triumph and faces no adversaries in his party. Leading a minority government with the continual prospect of defeat on the one hand and the tantalizing possibility of a majority on the other, he has been able to count on election-ready discipline in his caucus. But he too will lose his grip sooner or later. The fault, dear reader, is in our MPs, not in our institutions, that they are underlings.

Vanity Legislation

The fondest dream of many MPs is to get a private member's bill passed. A succession of procedural reforms have been adopted to make this easier. They amount to a Charter for vanity legislation. The rule changes may get a bit more publicity for MPs who introduce private member's bills. They will not give backbench MPs more power or lead to better legislation.

The argument for private member's bills is that they give more power to individual MPs. But individual MPs cannot pass any legislation. Parties were formed to bring together like-minded MPs to form a majority that could pass a coherent legislative program. When they win an election they form a government, and the government controls the agenda in the Commons.

Three hundred and eight members cannot all – or even most of them cannot – lay bills before their 307 colleagues and hope to have them thoughtfully considered and voted on. There simply is not time. It does not stop them trying. By the time the House of Commons rose for its summer recess on 22 June 2006, having first met on 3 April, 149 private member's bills had been introduced. The government had introduced only 23 bills.

Most private member's bills are simply a gesture. Perhaps they get a bit of attention for an issue, but it cannot be thought that they should ever be seriously considered by the House, let alone passed. The impossibility of dealing with them all is addressed by choosing a couple of dozen by lot to be dealt with in the maximum of five hours, usually less, set aside each week for private members' business. About four or five are passed each session. Most deal with subjects such as changing the name of the riding of Battle Creek to Westlock–St Paul. The National Organ Donor Week Act reads in its entirety, 'Throughout Canada, in each and every year, the last full week of April shall be known under the name of "National Organ Donor Week."' It took Liberal MP Dan McTeague three years to get his bill passed. It may get a bit more publicity for a worthy cause. It got McTeague a tiny bit of publicity. Publicity is all that private member's bills are about.

The few measures of substance passed result mainly from the indulgence of members. Svend Robinson was allowed to add sponsorship of the addition of sexual orientation to the bases of hate crime to his egregious record of public service.

There is often less to bills that pass than appears. Conservative MP John Duncan got a bill to eliminate excise tax on jewellery passed just days before the Martin government was defeated in November 2005. The Liberal budget introduced in February had begun to phase out the tax. Duncan's advocacy over several years helped get rid of the tax and in the distracted Thirty-eighth Parliament he was able to get it eliminated completely, but his luck in the private member's bill draw was a small factor in eliminating an obsolete tax.

Minority governments provide opportunities for mischievous private member's bills. Bill C-288, which requires the government to meet Kyoto targets, was passed both on the basis that it was about the most important legislation Parliament has ever passed and that it was meaningless. It was introduced by a Liberal MP to save the world and allowed to proceed by the Speaker on the grounds that it did not require the spending of money, which can be true only if it is meaningless. The Harper government unsuccessfully strove to have it defeated or at least delayed, but both the government and the opposition who supported it refused to see it as a matter of confidence, confirming that it was meaningless.

Private members have always been entitled to introduce bills. But any really bright ideas they might have would be taken up by the government and introduced by the relevant Cabinet minister. Such private member's bills as get passed are either trivial or an indulgence by the government of the sponsoring member's vanity. That was true before the rule changes and it will be true after them. On any issue of substance the government must have its way.

The rules now provide that private member's bills introduced in one session of Parliament can be picked up again where they left off in a new session, instead of having to be introduced again. The reporting when the new rules were passed claimed that this would mean that the government could no longer kill a bill by proroguing Parliament – as if the government would prorogue parliament to kill a private member's bill. As it is, parliamentary sessions are getting longer, and the rule change simply accepts that any private member's bill with a chance of getting passed is going to take years.

The rules also provide that a private member's bill shall be deemed passed by whatever committee it is referred to if has not been dealt with within sixty sitting days of its being referred to a committee by the House. As private member's bills of any substance are often responses to gusts of public anxiety and particularly in need of careful consideration in committee, this provision risks propelling a number of half-baked measures before the whole House.

Backbench MPs are not without influence. But that influence is mostly exercised privately, in party caucuses. There they have to be team players and can get no public recognition. It is not enough for some. More scope for private member's bills is only an indulgence of MPs' vanity. It will do little harm. It will do no good.

9 Cross-Purposes: Parliamentary Confirmation of Appointments

Confirmation

The reform most obviously fuelled by a desire to ape American models is parliamentary confirmation of government appointments. Canadians would not be saying that they want parliamentary confirmation of appointments to the Supreme Court of Canada if they had not been entertained by the spectacle of confirmation of Supreme Court appointments by the United States Senate.

The system of government provided for by the United States Constitution, for good or ill, largely for ill, is entirely different from Canada's. The president serves his term whether Congress likes it or not, and Congress cannot be dissolved to seek one that may work better with the president. Somehow or other, president and Congress must get along, and political culture and conventions have grown up to allow that they do, just.

The commonplace theory of the U.S. Constitution is that executive and legislative powers are separated. That is impossible, even in theory, and in several areas the Constitution requires that Congress and the president both participate in an action. So, in what seems the executive role of appointing officers, Congress, specifically the Senate, is involved. The Senate cannot chose officers itself but it must approve the president's choices, most notably his Cabinet choices.

The overwhelming number of presidential appointments are confirmed with little or no controversy, including obvious patronage appointments, such as agreeable ambassadorships for prominent supporters of the president. Confirmation battles, when they occur, are pure partisan politics. Some minor failings in the past or sharp-edged opinions are made into big political issues in an attempt to embarrass the president. The nominee may be excellent, and much less qualified people may have been nodded through their confirmations. Nominees are rarely rejected, a fuss being usually all that partisan politics demands.

The president's party often does not have a majority in the Senate and even a minority under the Senate's arcane rules can hold up appointments almost indefinitely but, practically, all appointments are confirmed with the connivance of contraries. In the end, the convention is that the president should have serve under him those he thinks best.

And that is the fundamental objection to parliamentary confirmation. It is part of government to choose who will serve in government. The opposition may not like the choices. Why should they? They see things differently and judge people differently. Their task is to persuade people to the let them govern. Then they can choose the people they think best. It should not be to try to prevent the government from governing and choosing the people to serve in government it thinks best. If that is not what it comes down to, what criteria should Parliament be applying in confirming appointments and what reason is there to think Parliament could apply them well?

When Frank McKenna appeared before a parliamentary committee on his appointment as ambassador to Washington, he was asked for his opinions on U.S.–Canada relations. For the position he had accepted, his opinions were irrelevant. He was to act as the government instructed him. Perhaps it was a test of his knowledge of the issues. But a parliamentary committee is hardly the forum for a foreign service exam. His main qualification for the job, why he was going, rather than a career diplomat, was that he had the confidence of the government and could speak to Washington with that confidence. That settled the matter. What MPs thought of him, and most thought he was a fine fellow, one of their club of politicians, was irrelevant.

If appointments were regularly subject to parliamentary confirmation, they would most likely all be nodded through by the government majority. Opposition MPs would make some partisan noise, but however 'free' MPs were, it would imply a complete lack of confidence in the government if MPs of the governing party were to vote against their government's nominee. Who gets to chair the CBC might not, in itself, seem an issue of confidence, but to spurn the choice of the government they purport to support on such a choice would imply a distinct lack of confidence.

Were parliamentary confirmation made routine, then, it might not make a great deal of difference. Those who dream that Alfonso Gagliano would not have been appointed ambassador to Denmark would be disappointed, and the damage suffered by the government for such a stupid appointment might be no more than it was. The risk is that making every appointment a potential political football will limit appointees to those with the tough political hides to bear up and will tend to bring forward those whose talents are political rather than administrative, diplomatic, judicial, or whatever may be required for the job.

The aborted appointment of Gwyn Morgan to chair a new Public Appointments Commission gave an unpleasant taste of what parliamentary confirmation could lead to. The commission was an innovation of the Harper government intended to assure that the process leading to public appointments would produce qualified candidates. It was not actually to make appointments or even assess individual candidates. The legislation creating the commission had not been passed when Morgan appeared before a Commons committee in May 2006 in a gesture towards reform. The Liberals and New Democrats ganged up to attack Morgan as a racist by misconstruing remarks he had made in a speech and rejected his nomination. Harper in a fit of pique dropped plans for the commission.

The commission was pointless, window dressing to appeal the whingers. But Morgan was an obviously distinguished and disinterested individual rejected out of pure politics. The remarks his critics seized on were impolitic, but normal people make impolitic remarks. Only politicians generally manage to avoid them.

Morgan's rejection came under procedures that have been part of the Standing Orders of the House of Commons since 1989.[71] They provide that the relevant Commons committee is notified of all appointments and may call the appointee before the committee within thirty days. The government may, as was done in Morgan's case, notify committees of its intention to appoint someone before making an appointment, giving the committee a chance to have a say in advance. But the committees have no power. The government can go ahead with an appointment in the face of committee opposition.

In the case of Morgan, the Harper government dropped the appointment and the office to which he was to be appointed. In the case of Glen Murray, a former mayor of Winnipeg who stepped down to run for the Liberals in 2004 and was defeated, Paul Martin had already appointed him head of the National Round Table on the Environment and the

Economy when he appeared before the Commons Committee on Environment and Sustainable Development in March 2005. The opposition members ganged up to pass a motion calling on Martin to withdraw the appointment. The objection to Murray boiled down to his being a Liberal. The implication of the opposition vote was that Murray had been appointed purely to give a plum to a Liberal. Whether that was true or not, the opposition members voted against his appointment purely to spite the Liberals.

The Murray and Morgan cases showed the incoherence of the confirmation argument. To keep politics out of appointments, more politics is brought in. It cannot work. As the American experience shows, confirmation cannot take politics and patronage out of appointments.

The cases also show that parliamentary confirmation during a minority government would be particularly unsatisfactory in the absence of the experience and conventions that keep government going in Washington. The combined opposition could reject all government appointments and plausibly maintain that they were not issues of confidence.

Public proceedings on appointments must either distort them with partisanship or settle down to a rather empty routine. Municipal councils that actually have the legal power to make many appointments regularly do so in camera.

Part of the impetus for parliamentary confirmation is a misplaced and exaggerated concern about patronage. It is a popular prejudice that politicians use appointments to give cushy jobs to their friends. They will, of course, tend to appoint people from their party, or at least not to appoint people from other parties. Why not? Liberals should think Liberals see things correctly and not be so sure about Conservatives and New Democrats. They might respect the integrity of people in other parties but think them wrong headed and unfit for public office. And politicians from one party might think that members of another party have not the wrong principles but no principles at all. So governments will naturally and rightly turn to their own in making appointments, and if you do not like that, you cannot like the government. The remedy is to throw the bums out, not to keep all governments from doing what they think best.

It would be no answer to restrict appointments to people who had not been politically active in any party. Political activity is a fundamental right and should not be a bar to a public appointment. If it were, political appointments could become the privilege of those who dissemble their political leanings in pursuit of appointments, and of those Kim

Campbell memorably described as 'condescending sons of bitches,' too proud to engage in the partisan fray.

The call for parliamentary confirmation of appointments is another case of reformers unhappy with government wanting to keep governments from governing. Government consists of myriad daily decisions. Appointments are only one category of decisions, not the most important, but attract attention because people are interesting and because, usually wrongly, they are supposed to be plums. The attempt to take power away from governments risks immobilizing them or diffusing and confusing responsibility until it passes beyond any control.

Advocates of parliamentary confirmation may say that they do not want to take the power to make appointments from government but simply to broaden participation in it, make it more open, and keep an eye on it. Parliament does not have the time to participate effectively in appointments, only to make an occasional partisan fuss. Only a tiny proportion of the people appointed by governments have been called before Commons committees since 1989. A public political process destroys the confidentiality necessary in hiring and rather than taking the politics out of appointments surcharges it, forcing every appointee to be a politician. We can keep an eye on appointments without parliamentary confirmation. They are announced. Any questionable appointments can be made an issue of.

If parliamentary confirmation became effective, in the sense that governments could not count on confirmation and had to make appointments to please MPs, even MPs of the government party who did not hold office, the responsibility of the government would be eroded. If an official confirmed by Parliament turned out badly, the government could fairly say, 'Don't blame us. We had a better candidate but could not be sure of confirmation.' And to whom would appointees be answerable: to the government whose second or third choices they were or to Parliament who confirmed them? The line of authority in government is from Cabinet, through ministers, to officials. That authority, and the responsibility that flows from it, would be weakened and confused if officials owed their appointments as much to MPs as to the government.

Crown corporations, the CBC for example, are supposed to be free of direct political control by the government. It would not assure their independence from politics to make appointments to them subject to public political wrangling. Suspicion of political patronage in Crown corporations is particularly strong. It is suggested that their boards and executives should be chosen like those of ordinary business, the government keeping out of it. But if there is any reason for a corporation being a Crown corporation, and not privatized, Crown corporations are not ordinary businesses. Consequently their directors and executives may need a political facility and the confidence of the government that they are more likely to have if chosen by the government from people, likely compatible with the government party, they know and trust. Conversely, many qualified executives and directors would not serve a Crown corporation because it was an arm of government and would be less likely to do so if they risked becoming political footballs in some kind of parliamentary confirmation process.

Judge Not Lest Ye Be Judged

Like a bad penny, a bad idea keeps turning up. One such bad idea is that judicial appointments, at least Supreme Court appointments, should be subject to some kind of public political confirmation hearings on the American model. As often, even those who have thought Americans are bastards and their president a moron are entranced by this American model.

The call for an open political process for judicial appointments comes not only from the right, upset by the courts' striking down legislation and prescribing new legislation on the basis of their reading of Charter rights. Left-wing law professors often support the idea. This in itself should give us pause.

The question must be asked, what criteria should MPs empowered to confirm judges apply? If the criteria are personal integrity, independence, legal learning, and experience of the courts, these are not things that MPs are specially able to assess, particularly in public. Nor can it be argued that the present system has failed by these criteria. Indeed many advocates of parliamentary confirmation of judges have no complaint with the appointments actually made but argue that confirmation is needed because there is a public perception that judges are somehow illegitimately chosen.[72] The perception is cultivated largely by those lobbying for confirmation. They sneer at the 'secret' process by which judges are chosen, but they do not question their qualifications. The truer word would be *confidential*, confidentiality being always necessary when appointments are being made. First choices may decline, and why should we and the second choice know that? Inquiries, perhaps security checks, must be made, and they can hardly be done publicly.

It is not in the government's interest to appoint dodgy lawyers to the bench. There are plenty of other patronage appointments for rewarding friends. As things stand, judicial prospects are discretely vetted and the results are about as good as we can hope.

The commonest justification for an open political process for judicial appointments is democratic control. Judges now make and unmake our laws with no thought of the voters. On this basis, the criterion for choosing a judge is whether he or she will decide cases in line with what politicians, as the voice of the people, want. This criterion faces both theoretical and practical difficulties.

What are judges for if they are simply to give us what we want? It is Parliament's job to give us what we want. The courts' role under the Charter is from time to time to tell us that we cannot have it. Whether the courts should have that role is another question. It will not be resolved by changing the way judges are appointed.

Judges on the Supreme Court of Canada often serve for fifteen to twenty years. Practically, it is impossible to anticipate what questions they may be asked to deal with in their careers on the bench. Would anyone have thought to ask for a nominee's position on gay marriage at a confirmation hearing in 1987? If he or she had dismissed the idea then, what guarantee would that have been for the judgment the Court would give on the Chrétien government's reference on the question in 2004? A nominee could quite honestly have answered a hypothetical question one way in 1987 and another way as a judge seventeen years later. In 1999 the Liberal government led an overwhelming majority of the House of Commons in supporting a resolution declaring that marriage was the union of a man and a woman. By 2005 the Liberal government was pridefully enacting the contrary. Why should judges publicly confirmed by politicians be any more consistent?

Most sitting judges when, rarely, they venture an opinion are against a public political process for appointing judges. Many of the best judges are modest people, shy of publicity. A public appointments process would put off many of the best candidates for the bench. Ambitious lawyers keen to cut a swath through the law would positively relish the limelight of a confirmation hearing and be politic enough to survive it.

Appointment to the Supreme Court of Canada is not the plum many people think it is. At any given time there are several judges on the provincial courts of appeal who would make fine judges on the Supreme Court but do not want to go to Ottawa. Making candidates political footballs would even further reduce the talent pool.

Despite its obvious dangers, a public political process for judicial appointments appeals to many leftists who set great store by judicial activism. They would be happy to answer the question by what right do judges tell us what laws we can and should make by saying that judges were publicly chosen by our elected representatives and have every right to be even more active than they have been. Once politic judges had been safely confirmed, they could even more take their cues from the ideologues in the law schools, and those not happy with their decisions could be told to exercise their constitutional right to shut up.

We have now had two goes at some kind of parliamentary vetting of Supreme Court appointments. When Rosalie Abella and Louise Charron were appointed, Justice Minister Irwin Cotler appeared before an ad hoc committee of MPs before Parliament had opened to tout their qualifications. MPs wanting to grill the candidates were frustrated, and nothing was accomplished except to whet the appetite for the real thing.

Most significantly this thin end of the wedge of the politicization of judicial appointments coincided with the appointment of Abella, the most political appointment yet. Abella, an undistinguished judge though first appointed to a low court at age twenty-nine, had spent much of her time since on leave from the bench on boards and commissions, notably a Royal Commission on Employment Equity. On previous Ontario vacancies on the Supreme Court, a journalistic claque had promoted her claims, to her cost perhaps. A frank promoter of judicial law-making[73] and of conventionally progressive views, Abella is just the sort of judge who would have weathered well-founded attacks on her fitness, with the enthusiastic support of progressive elites.

For the appointment of Marshall Rothstein, another ad hoc committee of MPs was assembled before Parliament had opened. On a short list left over from the Liberal government and already 'secretly' vetted by a committee with all party and legal and lay representation, Rothstein was a safe choice from every point of view.

The televised three-hour committee hearing was preceded by a short talk, what the *Globe and Mail* called a lecture,[74] by law professor Peter Hogg in which the committee members were told in no uncertain terms what they should and should not ask Rothstein. They were not to ask him about any judgments he had rendered and any he might have to render on the Supreme Court. They were not to ask him what he thought of same-sex marriage. Fatuously Hogg suggested 'six qualities that you might want to explore in your questioning.'

1. He must be able to resolve difficult legal issues, not just by virtue of technical legal skills, but also with wisdom, fairness and compassion.
2. He must have the energy and discipline to diligently study the materials that are filed in every appeal.
3. He must be able to maintain an open mind on every appeal until he has read all the pertinent material and heard from counsel on both sides.
4. He must always treat the counsel and the litigants who appear before him with patience and courtesy.
5. He must be able to write opinions that are well written and well reasoned.
6. He must be able to work cooperatively with his eight colleagues to help produce agreement on unanimous or majority decisions, and to do his share of the writing.[75]

How were they to figure out whether Rothstein had these qualities in a public hearing?

Despite intimations from MPs that they would ask Rothstein about issues, MPs did as they were told. Rothstein made politic remarks about judicial restraint and leaving Parliament to its work that, however honest and candid, were practically meaningless.

Some have suggested that without discussing specific cases past or hypothetical and without pretending to make a public character assessment, the committee could inquire into a candidate's jurisprudence or philosophy of law. The suggestion that MPs are qualified to do this and that the public would gain by it is ludicrous. It rests on a misconception in any event. All judges may have a philosophy of law just as we all have a metaphysics, without knowing it. But you can be an excellent judge without being able to talk intelligently about jurisprudence for two minutes. You just find the facts without prejudice and make sense of the applicable cases and legislation and the Charter as best you can. If we could successfully examine judges on their jurisprudence, what should we make of it? Would we be looking for Austinian positivists, legal realists, followers of Ronald Dworkin, wherever he might lead? The people best qualified to handle such questions are a small set of law professors quite unfit by their conceit, irresponsibility, and casuistry for any bench.

As judges are not to work with government and may have to judge it or its friends, partisanship in judicial appointments raises other issues. Partisanship and patronage have largely been removed from judicial appointments. Academics and others with an interest in the issue still occasionally squawk, but while it was taken for granted fifty years ago that Liberals would appoint Liberals to the bench and Conservatives Conservatives, it came to be less and less so, and procedures formalized under Mulroney keep partisan input to a minimum. Whether these procedures produce the best judges is another issue beyond the scope of this book. Whatever the professors may say, the bench has not markedly improved.

When Michel Bastarache unexpectedly stepped down in the spring of 2008, Stephen Harper had to appoint his second judge to the Supreme Court of Canada. Ever the politician, he set up a Supreme Court selection panel of two Tory MPs and one MP from each of the opposition parties. To what? To have a say? The legal power of appointment lies with the governor general in council, in effect the Cabinet, and it would require a constitutional amendment to change that. Whatever practices might be adopted to assure that all prospects are considered fairly, the appointment cannot be delegated to a committee of MPs, and the prime minister must be held responsible for the appointment.

The Bloc and NDP members of the panel complained that the two Tory members were Cabinet ministers 'who owe their jobs to Prime Minister Stephen Harper.'[76] In more than three months the panel got nowhere, and on 5 September 2008 Harper scrapped it and announced his intention to appoint Thomas Cromwell, who had been appointed straight from practice to the Nova Scotia Court of Appeal by Jean Chrétien in 1997. Harper said there would be another televised vetting by an ad hoc committee of MPs.

Despite Cromwell's being hailed as a 'dream candidate,' Professor Peter Russell 'blasted the federal move. "Did they draw Cromwell's name out of a hat?"'[77] and NDP MP Joe Comartin, who had for three months been playing politics on the panel and vainly imagining that he would appoint the next judge of the Supreme Court of Canada, complained that 'we have a Prime Minister and a justice minister playing politics with Supreme Court appointments' while acknowledging that Cromwell was eminently qualified for the job.[78]

Short one judge, the nine-member Supreme Court had been sitting in panels of seven to avoid the possibility of a tie for several months when Harper finally appointed Cromwell on 22 December 2008. The election and the uproar over the coalition and the prorogation had sidelined the public vetting charade, but Harper spoke to Michael Ignatieff, who sensibly concurred in the appointment.

The Supreme Court selection panel was a step beyond American practice, where there is no procedure restricting the president in nominations to the courts and only Senate confirmation after nomination. But, like confirmation, it served only to politicize and delay an important function of government.

As there is not likely to be another vacancy for some years, we have time to reflect and step back from the folly.

10 Perpetual Elections: Recall

Many people do not like their MP. Their MP has done things or said things they do not like. They have a low opinion of politicians generally. They voted for another candidate.

Some people think that their MP should be just the tool of the voters, always doing exactly what they want, as if that could be continually determined.

Whether they just do not like their MP or because their idea of the MP's role entails that members should forfeit their seats for insubordination, some people cannot wait for the next election to get rid of their MP. They want to be able to recall her.

Several of the United States have recall legislation, though it has seldom been effectively used. California's recall of Governor Gray Davis in 2003 was a headline-grabbing exception. It was the first successful recall of a California governor, after thirty-two tries, and only the second recall of any state governor, the last to fall being the governor of North Dakota in 1921.

British Columbia has pioneered this reform too and passed the first[79] and still only recall legislation in the Commonwealth in 1995. It provides that if a petition signed by 40 per cent of the registered voters in a riding can be produced in sixty days, the member will be unseated and a by-election held. No petition can be started until eighteen months after an election. Any grounds for recall may be asserted, in 200 words or less. Twenty petitions have been started but most were dropped and none have succeeded. One MLA, Paul Rietsma, who had made an ass of himself writing letters to local newspapers under assumed names and been kicked out of the Liberal Caucus, resigned as a petition picked up steam in June 1998.

The British Columbia Civil Liberties Association launched a Charter challenge to the recall legislation on the plausible grounds, amongst others, that it infringes on a citizen's right to vote because a recall petition is not a secret ballot and because the votes of those not signing a petition are not counted. They did not pursue the case as the interest in and threat of recall faded.

The particular faults of any specific recall legislation all stem from the folly of the idea. In the United States recall is typically a two- or three-stage process, in which a petition requiring the signatures of 25 per cent or less of the voters triggers a general vote on recall, followed by, or held with, the election of a replacement. In some cases only specified grounds for recall can be asserted.

Whatever the rules, recall amounts to an opening for perpetual elections.

This is obscured by the confusion of recall's supporters and the ambiguity of the proceedings. Is recall disciplinary or political? If the grounds for unseating a member are an offence, from murder to corruption, or conflict of interest, or lack of attendance, or incapacity, it should be a matter for the courts or the House. Through Parliament's long history MPs acquired privileges and immunities to protect them from intimidation by the Crown and private interests. These remain and they remain necessary. But legal grounds for unseating an MP do not require recall. The Criminal Code, for instance, provides that a member loses his seat if convicted of an offence carrying a sentence of more than two years' imprisonment.

The real impetus behind recall is political. The ambiguity of the proceedings encourages petitioners to hype political differences into offences. Recall petitions may assert that a member has lied, or misled the voters, or has betrayed them or abused her position. But the arguments over recall are no different from the arguments in an election and the question is the same: 'Do you want this person to be your MP or another?'

The one big difference in a recall fight is that the choice in an election is between a known fixed set of candidates. In a recall fight, the sitting member is up against an unknown opponent, perhaps the candidate of the petitioners' dreams. Some American states try to overcome this by combining a recall vote with the election of a successor, but this brings its own awkwardnesses. The candidates are running in a hypothetical election, for there may be no vacancy. Or the two votes are conflated and it becomes simply another election, triggered by the petition of a small fraction of the voters.

The argument that an MP should be unseated if he does not do what the voters want falls first on the fact that it can never really be known what the voters want. We elect representatives because we cannot, as a mass of voters, make all the decisions of which government consists. This is not just because we do not have the time or knowledge, or because of difficulties of communication, but also because of the impossibility of aggregating preferences that leads to the paradox of voting.

Even when there are known majority opinions of the voters, on one or another issue voters and their MP may be at odds, but issues cannot be taken in isolation. Most voters know on election day that the candidate they will vote for stands for some things they do not like. No candidate can be in perfect agreement with any voter but himself. Demanding that MPs be recalled for crossing the voters on any single issue amounts to recall for insubordination. Demanding perfect obedience from an MP makes him a slave to a master whose will cannot be known. And if voters will cut him a little slack, how many disagreements must there be or how weighty must the issues be before an MP can justly be recalled? Any answer to these questions is lost in the general question whether the voters still want the sitting member to be their MP.

Moreover, the doctrine that an MP should do only exactly what the voters want is far from universally held. A member may have been elected by voters who believe in Edmund Burke's theory of representation.[80] It would not be fair to expose her to recall for offending a doctrine to which she and many who voted for her had not subscribed.

Recall then can only amount to asking the voters between elections the pollsters' question 'If an election were held today would you vote for …?' and making the hypothetical question actual. With the last election two years past and the next election two years off, the petitioners organize another election.

Elections are the heart of democracy, but they are a means and not an end, and neither MPs nor voters can be perpetually in elections. The MP has a job to do. The voters have lives to live. MPs are perhaps too continually wooing the voters as it is, and voters are not keen to have politicians after them any more than necessary.

Recall legislation, as experience in the United States has shown, may not make much difference to our politics. The novelty wore off and the difficulty of recall sank in, and there have been no new petitions in British Columbia since April 2003. But it is not an argument for a reform that it will be ineffective. It must be judged by what its effects might be if it were regularly in operation. As it is, recall has been a distraction in British Columbia politics and a waste of money and energy.

Proponents of recall generally argue that the burden on the promoters of a recall is too onerous, whether in the number of supporters required or the time limits or formalities. But the easier it is to start the process, the greater the likelihood that it will be used as a distraction when there is no chance of actually unseating the incumbent. The longer it is allowed to go on, the greater the likelihood that people will change their minds. At a limit we could imagine Internet polls done daily. A member could be out Tuesday and back on Friday. Being recalled is not usually, and should not be, a disqualification from running again. To disqualify a citizen from running for public office is a draconian penalty, a gross infringement of the political rights not only of the disqualified politician but of the voters.

Some argue[81] that recall can strengthen the ties of a member to his riding and strengthen the standing of a member by making the threat of recall a counterpoise to party discipline. But it is no nobler to be a slave of the voters than to be a slave of a party. As the British Columbia experience indicates, members are as likely to be the target of a recall campaign because of their prominence in government or a party as for signally failing or offending voters in their riding. Half the recall petitions in British Columbia targeted a Cabinet minister or party leader. Gordon Campbell was a target both when he was leader of the opposition and after he became premier.

There is a telling disproportion between the enthusiasm for recall, backed by over 80 per cent of the voters in a referendum held with the 1991 British Columbia general election, still talked up by academics, journalists, and reform lobbies and earnestly offered by Elections BC, and British Columbia's dead letter legislation. What seemed so simple and appealing turns out to be an otiose complication.

The thoughtlessness combined with keenness for ingenious technicalities characteristic of reform is most striking if one asks how recall would work with the STV. Many in British Columbia, evidently, are keen on both. But as a member in a five-member riding under STV can be elected with less than 17 per cent of the vote, what would be required for a recall? Eighty-three per cent of the voters might want a recall the morning after the election. Consider that a member may have needed sixth and seventh preferences to get elected, some of them fractional votes, and the question who elected the member and who should be able to recall her becomes unfathomable.

Hard Cases

Two hard cases, Jag Bhaduria in 1994 and David Emerson in 2006, will have tempted people to support bad law.

In Jag Bhaduria's case, the voters of Markham undoubtedly elected an MP at the low end of the range of competence and integrity found in MPs. He had embellished his résumé and been fired in 1990 as a teacher with the Toronto Board of Education for writing threatening letters to school administrators. But nothing had changed after the 1993 election. The voters had not being paying attention. The Liberals who nominated him had not been paying attention. He had even run before, in 1988, gaining almost 22,000 votes. We should all pay closer attention to candidates, particularly the parties, who will suffer if they put up a wrong un. The Liberals managed to lose Markham in 1997, one of only two seats they lost in Ontario that year. But recall as a remedy for voter inattention is no argument. If the voters will not pay attention to an election, they are even less likely to pay attention to a recall fight.

Had recall been available, David Emerson might well have been the first MP recalled. But what would have been the point of that except to enforce a rule that members should not cross the floor, which I have earlier argued would be a bad rule? On the day he joined the Conservative Cabinet Emerson was as good or bad, as able or not, as on the day he was re-elected. The wrong was more Stephen Harper's in taking him into his Cabinet than Emerson's.

If recall legislation like that adopted in British Columbia had been in effect in Ottawa, no recall petition could have been launched until the summer of 2007. Even if recalled, Emerson would have had some twenty months to render such service to the state as he fancied and would have served Harper's purpose. He was never likely to seek re-election, and it was bound to be a short Parliament. Indeed Emerson was reportedly unhappy that it lasted as long as it did.[82]

The Bhaduria and Emerson cases illustrate the ambiguity of recall. Is it a kind of judgment against the member for an offence or simply a chance for the voters to change their minds? Those who wanted Emerson unseated thought he had broken a fundamental rule, but if there should be a rule against crossing the floor, the rule should be enforced by the House of Commons or the courts and not by the voters acting as prosecutor, judge, and jury all in one.

Those who wanted Bhaduria unseated had changed their minds after learning things about him they could have known before the election. In a happier if fanciful case, voters might want a recall because Wayne Gretzky had shown up in the riding interested in running and the voters could not wait for the next election.

11 Do It Yourself: Initiative

In the second decade of the last century, under the influence of the Progressive movement in neighbouring states,[83] all the Western provinces passed acts providing for what was generally called direct legislation, or initiative. Manitoba's Initiative and Referendum Act was declared unconstitutional by the Judicial Committee of the Privy Council in 1919 and no actual legislation was ever voted on under the acts, though Alberta's remained on the books until it was repealed in 1958 after some voters made enquiries as to how it would work.

In 1995 British Columbia revived initiative legislation in Canada in the same act that brought in recall. Under this legislation, a voter can submit a draft bill to the chief electoral officer, and a petition is issued. The proponent has ninety days to get the signatures of 10 per cent of the registered voters in each of British Columbia's eighty-five ridings. If the necessary signatures are gathered, the bill is submitted to a committee of the legislature, and the legislature may, if it sees fit, pass it. If the legislature does not pass the bill, it is put to a vote and, if 50 per cent of registered voters and 50 per cent of the registered voters in two thirds of the ridings vote in favour, the initiative vote is declared 'successful.' The legislation provides for voting on initiatives on the last Saturday of September in every third year from 1999.

Because under the Constitution Act the province cannot take legislative power away for the lieutenant governor in the assembly – the point that was fatal to the Manitoba legislation in 1919 – the legislation simply provides that the proposed bill must be introduced in the legislature after a 'successful' vote: much ado for very little, it would seem, though, in the extremely unlikely event of a 'successful' initiative vote, the legislature would be unlikely to turn down the bill.

Only six petitions were started from 1995 to 2002, on subjects as various as a proportional representation electoral system, an act to prohibit the hunting of bears, and an act to balance the budget and retire provincial debt. None got anywhere near the required number of signatures for submission to a committee of the legislature. For eight years the legislation seemed a dead letter.

Initiative is the reductio ad absurdum of reform. Despairing of getting the governments they elect to do what they want, the voters will take matters into their own hands and draft and adopt their own legislation. In practice it is impossible for there to be in Canada a groundswell of support for a measure sufficient for a successful initiative that would be ignored by government. The government would enact the demanded measure before the initiative could be completed. Only to humour the enthusiasts would it stand back and let the initiative take its course.

American examples are no evidence to the contrary. The irresponsible congressional governments of the United States, with their separation of powers between the executive and the legislature, and their checks and balances in full operation, can fail to enact popular measures, though successful initiatives have been rare in the United States. Oregon, where direct legislation originated, has had an unusual number from local pride in the institution and because the Oregon Constitution contains an unusual number of substantive provisions that would be legislation in other jurisdictions.

Like recall, initiative, where allowed, is not likely to be much used or to get very far. But if it did get off the ground, it would be a bad thing. It involves taking a single issue in isolation out of the hands of government without regard to how the promoted measure may sort with the rest of what government is doing. If it turns out badly, who will be held responsible? Whatever the specific initiative legislation, if it were to take hold, there would be a tendency to think that what the people had wrought only the people should undo, requiring a laborious further initiative to amend or repeal bad legislation adopted by initiative, instead of the quick second thoughts possible with ordinary legislation. Legislation passed in the ordinary way is often amended many times as it goes through the various stages in Parliament or a provincial assembly. Legislation promoted in an initiative, possibly drafted by amateurs, could not receive any fine-tuning.

As is now de rigueur when there is to be voting, initiative legislation comes packed with provisions to regulate campaigning and the financing of campaigning. It is one thing to regulate elections and election financ-.

es when the issue is whether Jones or Lee or Scarpia is to be elected. It is another thing to try to regulate all discussion of a political issue once it becomes the subject of an initiative. It cannot be effectively done, but the attempt would involve serious interference with free public debate.

British Columbia's requirements both for the calling of an initiative vote and for a 'successful' vote are high and objected to by the enthusiasts for initiative. But to lower the requirement for calling a vote would risk voters being continually harried by initiative campaigns with no hope of success. To lower the requirement for a 'successful' vote to a simple majority of those who vote would allow initiators to compel voters who want no part of their initiative to go to the polls to vote no.

Promoters of initiative have no difficulty in producing polls showing overwhelming support for it. It was even more strongly backed than recall in the 1991 British Columbia referendum. But the massive support in theory, together with the lack of impact in practice, shows that initiative is a pipe dream and shows how uncomprehending public support for reform can be.

The movement for direct legislation in the West was propelled by large non-partisan organizations, grain growers, prohibitionists, and unions that imagined that they could organize successful initiatives. Either they were wrong in imagining that what they wanted a majority must have wanted, or they found that they could get what they wanted through party politics and ordinary legislation, even if that meant forming new parties like the United Farmers and the Progressives. This more than the Judicial Committee of the Privy Council extinguished the enthusiasm for direct legislation.

There is a reason why we have parliaments. We can't do it ourselves. The Judicial Committee's apparently technical reason for quashing Manitoba's legislation has that substantive ground. Initiative tries to set up an ad hoc alternative legislature to be summoned whenever a significant number of voters work up enough steam to start a petition. But our institutions are responsive enough that no measure likely to win an initiative vote could not be more efficiently adopted by a legislature. And more importantly perhaps, they are responsible enough to be subject to correction by experience and elections. Support for initiative is just a way of venting our frustration that we can't always get what we want.

A Populist Veto?

After eight years as a dead letter, British Columbia's initiative legislation came back with a vengeance in the spring of 2010 as the popular hysteria against the Goods and Services Tax was ramped up by former Social Credit premier Bill Vander Zalm in an initiative campaign to repeal legislation to harmonize the Goods and Services Tax with British Columbia's sales tax. A surplus of signatures required for the initiative was easily obtained, and unless Gordon Campbell's Liberal government caves or some technical flaw is found in the petition, there will be a vote on an HST Extinguishment Act on 24 September 2011, fourteen months after the tax has been implemented. Campbell's hope must be that by that time British Columbia voters will be used to the tax and see that it is not the end of the world. Perhaps.

The use of initiative as a populist veto is a particular danger of the procedure. All governments must do unpopular things, particularly about taxes. The Harmonized Sales Tax is only obliquely a tax rise, because the Goods and Services Tax applies to more than British Columbia's sales tax, and, should it be repealed, ways will be found, particularly by a New Democratic government, to make up the loss of revenue. But the isolation of a tax measure from the whole of government's work is a telling example of the irresponsibility of initiative. The anti-HST campaign, those who sign the petition, and those who may vote for it, are beyond responsibility for the tax rises, spending cuts, or increased debt that their success would bring.

Moreover, the British Columbia government entered into a legally binding agreement with Ottawa for the Harmonized Sales Tax. If all government actions are subject to a populist veto, no government's word can be trusted.

And the encompassing of the Harmonized Sales Tax in an initiative campaign has involved British Columbia's chief electoral officer in an officious attempt to regulate public discussion of the issue. He came down against a government mailer on the budget that introduced the Harmonized Sales Tax.[84] The abuse of government information campaigns for partisan purposes is an issue beyond the scope of this book, but to explain something is usually to justify it, and the British Columbia government is obliged to explain the Harmonized Sales Tax as it is about to come into force, and any explanation is bound to counter the hysteria on which the anti-HST campaign is based. Perhaps the chief electoral officer will object to the publication of this book.

The anti-HST campaign, drawing on a populist reaction, is not a true citizens' initiative. It is driven by partisan politics. Its leader is a remnant of a practically defunct party. The NDP is vigorously engaged, as is the resuscitated British Columbia Conservative Party. Whatever the outcome, it is expected that Campbell and his finance minister will be targeted by recall campaigns. These are all moves in the 2013 election campaign. The NDP can repeal the Harmonized Sales Tax when they become the government, and take responsibility for the consequences.

Though this initiative is organized by politicians, the populist nature of initiative makes compromise difficult. If Campbell's were a minority government, or he faced a back bench revolt, he could try to compromise with opponents of the Harmonized Sales Tax legislation. But how does one compromise with upwards of fifty thousand signatories of a petition who have gone on to other things. A successful petition is a juggernaut that can only be stopped by the initiative bill being introduced in the legislature. There it could be defeated or amended beyond recognition, but it would be a brave government that tried that gambit, however well intentioned.

If initiative were to develop into a populist veto, we should see governments shying away from anything unpopular and no one to blame but ourselves when it all goes wrong. California teetering on the edge of bankruptcy offers a warning to British Columbia. We shall see.

Trick Questions

Initiative is a form of referendum distinguished by being, at least in theory, initiated by voters rather than politicians. Referendums have a long history in Canada. They were most commonly used to adopt and to remove local prohibition. There is something to be said for their use on constitutional issues, particularly if the voters can be counted on to say no.

Reformers have been keen to extend the use of referendums by requiring approval in a referendum for tax increases (in Ontario and Manitoba), and in Manitoba for the sale of Manitoba Hydro. The selection of a few issues for approval by referendum is a dishonest trick. While pretending simply to give the voters their say, those who promote such referendums plainly intend that the simple bother of a referendum, or the risk that opposition will well up over one issue in isolation, will make doing whatever requires referendum approval more difficult and unlikely. But why should tax increases be put to a vote and not spending cuts, or borrowing, or tax cuts? Under the guise of populism such reformers are simply trying to entrench their policies.

Happily such legislation may have little effect. When Dalton McGuinty's Liberal government in Ontario decided to raise taxes not long after they were elected promising not to raise them, they simply exempted themselves from the referendum requirement and it was hardly noticed.

12 The Senate

Like the proclamation of a new religion, from the late 1980s the call for a triple-E Senate rang out from the West. We narrowly escaped grotesque Senate reforms intended to answer the call when Meech Lake and Charlottetown were defeated.

The merits, effects, and workability of proposals for Senate reform were ignored in the constitutional negotiations in the compulsion to make a deal. Now Stephen Harper hopes, by indirection, to do as much damage as an almost unanimous previous generation of politicians could not do by direct constitutional amendment and again the merits, effects, and workability of his proposals are ignored. For Harper an elected Senate is both a proof of piety and a political ploy. An elected Senate has no merit, would have damaging effects on government and, at best, simply would not work.

Most countries have bicameral legislatures. How the members of the second house are chosen, and what its legal powers are, vary widely. The second house of a legislature is commonly called the upper house, implying special stature or dignity, but all second houses in parliamentary governments are in practice subordinate in power to the lower house. The last E in the triple E, equal, elected and *effective,* aims to cast off that subordination. It cannot, without destroying parliamentary government.

A Bit of History

The origin of upper houses has a rich history, but rather less significance for politics in the twenty-first century. Medieval kings summoned their subjects to assemblies in their various estates. In some countries there were as many as four houses: nobles, clergy, knights, and commoners. In England, which provided the model for parliaments the world over, including Continental Europe as it became democratic, the nobles and clergy sat in one house, the Lords, and country representatives, sometimes known at the knights of the shires, and representatives of the enfranchised towns sat in the other, the Commons. No one sat in Parliament or was represented simply as a subject or a citizen. It was property and status, the ability to provide money or service, that was represented in Parliament.

Though universal male suffrage was not complete in Britain (or Canada) until the twentieth century, by the nineteenth century the British House of Commons had become a popular assembly recognizably like the House of Commons in Ottawa today. The House of Lords was practically obliged to defer to it in most matters from the early eighteenth century. The Lords' formal powers were almost equal to those of the Commons until the Parliament Act of 1911. In practice there was always a way to get around the Lords, if it did not restrain itself. The King had unlimited power to create new peers. In a crisis he would do this on the advice of a government that commanded a majority in the Commons. The threat of new creations was enough to pass the Reform Bill in 1832 and the Parliament Act in 1911. In 1711 Queen Anne created twelve new Tory peers to overcome a Whig majority in the Lords that had been obstructing her Tory government's moves to make peace with France.

The House of Lords that the Fathers of Confederation knew when they were designing Canada's Parliament was not elected, or effective, or, in any respect, equal. It was defended and respected as the house of 'sober second thought,' where measures passed by the Commons were sometimes delayed or amended, and peers who had inherited their seats, and newly created peers who had distinguished themselves in one field or another, brought perspectives missing from the politics of the Commons. And it was supposed to defend property and be a bulwark against democratic excess.

All the colonies to be included in the new dominion had upper houses known as legislative councils. Two houses for Ottawa seemed natural. The allocation of seats by province was a useful bargaining chip in reconciling the colonies to their absorption in the new dominion. A property qualification, appointment for life, changed to age seventy-five in 1965, and the requirement that senators be at least thirty, almost middle age in the nineteenth century, encouraged the desired sobriety. The powers of the Senate were to be the same as the legal powers of the

Lords. But a provision for adding extra senators, a contrivance modelled on the Queen's power to create new peers, was added to keep the Senate in check. It has been used only once, as it was intended to be used, to overcome the antics of Liberal senators trying to block the GST in 1990.

During most of Canada's history the party in power has had a majority in the Senate. When it has not, the Senate has usually restrained itself, as the Lords did, from thwarting the will of the Commons. Popular government had become a universal faith by the late nineteenth century, and the Senate knew it would not survive if it attempted to exercise its full powers.

In 1856 the Province of Canada, a union of what are today Ontario and Quebec, amended its constitution to provide for elections to fill seats in its legislative council. By the eve of Confederation three-quarters of the legislative councillors had been elected for eight-year terms. But it made no difference. The government of the province was already at the impasse that impelled its leaders to seek Confederation. The elected legislative council simply reproduced the conflicts in the legislative assembly in miniature.

At Confederation, Ontario chose to do without a legislative council, while Quebec chose to return to an appointed council. One by one the legislative councils were abolished. Quebec's went last, in 1969. Only the Senate remains: usually forgotten, often abused, and an inviting target for reform.

E-E-E-K!

The unreflecting demand of a democratic age is that the Senate should be elected. As we already have an elected House of Commons, an elected Senate becomes the answer to all imagined failings in democracy as practised in the Commons. We could try proportional representation there, or allocate seats for women and minorities. The most popular idea is that it should in some sense represent the provinces. Whatever the justification for an elected Senate, it must be 'effective' to administer whatever corrective its advocates imagine government in Ottawa needs. Thus emerged the triple-E Senate, worshipped by the original members of the Reform Party. The provinces would have equal representation, the senators would be elected, and the reformed Senate would right all the wrongs done to the West and generally keep Ottawa under control.

The equal aspect of the triple-E Senate is the least important, even to true believers. No one really thinks that any good can come of giving Prince Edward Island the same number of seats in the Senate as British Columbia. They can only say, why not, if Rhode Island and California each have two seats in the United States Senate? The point of equality is to assure that the West gets a larger share of the Senate than it does of the Commons and that Ontario and Quebec get smaller shares. A vast over-representation of the Maritimes is an accident that might attract allies in the East. But it was always a non-starter, as Quebec will never agree to give up its over-representation.

Elected and effective go together in the minds of true believers. As Canada's experience shows, an unelected upper house, whatever its legal powers, must defer on all important matters to the elected lower house. But electing an upper house does not assure its 'effectiveness,' should that be desired. Very often the party that controls the lower house will also control the upper house, which will then follow its lead. Where a different method of electing the upper house – representation by region rather than population, indirect election, longer terms, a different electoral system – produces a different balance of forces in the upper house, its legitimacy and authority will suffer, regardless of its legal powers.

A government commanding a majority in the House of Commons has won the support of the largest bloc of voters. It may not, as electoral reformers never tire of pointing out, have won the votes of a majority, but it has the strongest claim to speak for the people. An elected Senate in conflict with the Commons must necessarily have a weaker claim to speak for the people. A distribution of Senate seats by region or province, without regard to population, would make possible a Senate majority elected by a small minority of voters. Whatever theory might have justified ignoring representation by population in the Senate, in practice minority rule through the Senate would not be tolerated. Similarly, if senators were distinguished from the Commons by longer, fixed terms, they could not easily stand against a more recently elected Commons exposed to the voters at any time.

Special Effects

But what if an elected Senate were effective? What if it retained its full legal powers and, buoyed by election, used them freely? There is a delusion among some on the right who say they favour more freedom through less government, that by making it more difficult to pass legislation an effective Senate would produce less government. The simplest reply to this argument is to point out that if passing new legislation would become more difficult, so would repealing old legislation become more difficult. You will not get less government by turning the Revised Statutes of Canada into the law of the Medes and the Persians.

Moreover, making it more difficult to pass legislation, giving a say on legislation to independent and conflicting bodies, need not lead to the passage of less legislation. It is as likely to lead to the passage of longer and more complicated legislation brokered to satisfy conflicting interests. If the result of conflict between the Commons and an effective Senate were brokered legislation, the result would likely be more government rather than less. Brokerage, involving special provisions and exemptions, leads to complication and a heavier load of government.

For reformers, an effective Senate would be the repository of all their hopes, the talisman against all their fears. It would have blocked the National Energy Policy. It would have stopped the GST, no matter that it is now universally agreed that the GST is a good thing, only cut by Harper in a cynical effort to buy votes. But the West's protection against another National Energy Policy is more seats in the House of Commons. And presumably Tory senators elected from Alberta would have voted as solidly for the GST at did Alberta Tories in the House of Commons.

This is the vague dreamy meaning of effectiveness in the minds of reformers. An upper house would be a 'check' against whatever they do not like. It would as likely stop whatever they might like.

It is a common error of reformers to seek in formal institutional change, whose consequences must be unpredictable, answers to concrete political concerns that can only be met by winning arguments and political organization. What would be the effect of any particular reform on specific political issues is unknowable. We can only know what its general effect on the ability of governments to act responsibly may be.

A truly effective Senate would subvert responsible government. It is the point of responsible government that with the confidence of a majority of the Commons it can tax and spend and legislate coherently according to its lights and be held responsible, first by the Commons and then by the voters. Were conflict between the Commons and the Senate to prevent that, government would be as heavy and intrusive as ever, but incapable of reacting to changing conditions and changing public opinion. And governments could neither take responsibility nor be held responsible when they could always say, 'We would have governed well, but the Senate would not let us.'

In the dream of reformers, an elected Senate would be filled by a better class of politician. Inevitably, however, elected senators would be party politicians. Parties would decide what the Senate would do. Would a Senate dominated by the opposition try to thwart a government commanding the House of Commons, perhaps after a recent election, or would it hold back, hoping to win a majority in the Commons, after the government had done its worst, at the next election? It would depend in part on how the different majority in the Senate had been elected. Was it longer terms, different dates for Senate elections, how the Senate seats were distributed, or a different electoral system that produced a different majority in the Senate? If it was a difference in timing that produced the different majority, those controlling the Senate could bide their time, making trouble but letting the government govern in the hope of governing themselves in time. If it was a different distribution of seats or a different electoral system that produced the different majority, there might be no prospect of bringing the houses together.

Whatever produced the situation, party politics would determine how the game was played out. A party that had lost the last Commons election would be trying to reverse the result through the Senate or to keep the government from governing.

Even the unelected Senate is deployed in the political game, as Harper has complained the Liberals have been doing, though what little of substance he has proposed was waved through the Liberal-dominated Senate. Senators might be blamed for blocking his Senate reforms, but for all his intermittent huffing and puffing he has not, as we shall see, figured out what he wants to do with the Senate. 'Partisan obstruction,' while it might be emboldened if senators were elected, would be no more 'legitimate' or 'justified.'[85]

Prior to Confederation, in the old Province of Canada, a convention emerged, once responsible government had been conceded, that governments should have a 'double majority.' Governments hoped for majority support in both Canada East and Canada West, as Quebec and Ontario were then known. The leaders of the majority in each half of the province were practically co-premiers, and governments were known by their names: Baldwin-Lafontaine, Hincks-Morin, Macdonald-Cartier, etc. The double majority convention proved unworkable. Governments were weak and unstable. Confederation was in large part designed to solve the problem double majorities could not. While creating the new Dominion of Canada, it split the old Canada, letting Quebec and Ontario govern themselves to a large extent.

An effective Senate could be a return to the days of the double majority. No government could be effective without a majority in both houses. When it was not forthcoming, there would be weak and unstable governments and possibly frequent elections to try for something better. We have recently had cheers for minority governments,[86] and so long at the Bloc Québécois holds on to its block of thirty or more seats in the House of Commons it seems an indefinite prospect, but an elected Senate offers the prospect of double minorities, which would be too much of what may not be a good thing.

The drive to have two effective houses of Parliament, like many reforms, aims to carry the conflicts of the voters unresolved into Parliament. The purpose of elections is to choose representatives who will support and hold accountable a government, and pass judgment on it, perhaps choose a new government. Elections should decide who governs. A Senate elected on a different basis from that of the Commons, or at a different time, would mean that the decision on government we are supposed to make in elections would be thwarted, by votes counted in a different way or at different times. If different electoral systems produced conflicting houses, the work of government would be paralyzed until one theory of elections prevailed.

Sitting Still

The worst that can be said of the unreformed Senate is that it is a waste of money. The news that another forgotten politician is to receive a good salary to age seventy-five and a nice pension after that for duties that are usually part time and may be scandalously shirked has traditionally excited general resentment. Senators' attempts to defend themselves by recounting the good work they do, particularly in committees, are ignored. The senators are right. They have knowledge, experience, and time, and can look at legislation more thoughtfully than MPs obsessed with cultivating their constituencies, desperate for a little publicity, and generally uninterested in the detail of what governments do.

In practice the Senate has only persuasive power. It cannot or will not defy a determined Commons. If in its deliberations it comes up with sensible amendments or appealing proposals, they may be accepted. When the Senate has been deployed politically to take a stand that the opposition controlling it hope will be popular, it is at its worst, as it demonstrated in the degraded show it put on in the fight against the GST. Senators could be an abler selection of Canadians. They would not be if they were elected. They would be just like MPs. They would be better if we chose to elect better governments.

The whining and sneering that has greeted each new set of Senate appointments for decades does not constitute intelligent criticism of the institution. It is the same resentment that wells up over all so-called patronage appointments. There will always be positions governments will have to fill with people of like mind and in whom they have confidence. And they will have to be paid. To a Conservative, all Liberal appointments may seem unworthy, because they are Liberal. But abstracting from partisanship, it must be acknowledged that to a Liberal they must seem perfectly respectable. This analysis will not satisfy the adherents of the 'They're all the same' party, but the TATS will not be satisfied. They have no more respect for elected politicians than appointed ones and would despise elected senators as much as they do appointed ones.

There is nothing stopping the government from reducing senators' pay and pensions and tying them more closely to attendance. Elected senators might plausibly argue for a pay increase and would need lavish equivalents of MPs' constituency offices and aides.

What's It For?

What are upper houses for? Why are they so common? The sheer inertia that has kept Canada's Senate going practically unchanged for 140 years and kept the House of Lords a majority hereditary body until 1999 (and has thwarted plans to reform it further since then) can also explain the persistence of upper houses in most countries. They provide a handy subject for academic study by political scientists, who may make up uses for them when none exist. But there are broadly two explanations, sometimes working together, for upper houses: to restrain democracy and to represent regions.

As democracy took hold in the nineteenth century, even when aristocratic upper houses no longer seemed acceptable, there was anxiety about what the newly empowered people might do, particularly to property. Upper houses would restrain popular excesses. The Senate of Canada's 'sober second thought' and its property qualification, made immaterial by general prosperity, indicate that this was one of its intended roles. But it is not a role that has life in it now. The general triumph of democracy, and its general sobriety, has prevailed even in upper houses and inhibits them, even when their inclinations might be to stand against the popular will expressed by a lower house and their legal powers would permit it.

The role of upper houses in representing regions has been no more effective. It can only matter when the regions represented in the upper house have greatly differing populations, requiring gross over-representation of voters in some regions and under-representation of voters in others. An upper house majority representing a small minority of voters will not be effective, whatever its legal powers may be.

The push for an elected Senate came largely from the West, feeling its voice was not heard in Ottawa. This is an issue that is fading as the West's population grows and redistribution gives it more seats in the Commons. The West already has greater representation in the Commons than it would have in a triple-E Senate. But the devotion to an elected Senate persists, though it could fade, if only the politicians would let it. Senate reform has taken on a life of its own. Piously included in the Conservative platform for three elections in which it was not an issue, Senate reform is brought forward as a show of promise keeping, whatever its merits and whether or not anyone cares or understands.

Messing About

Reaction to Stephen Harper's initiatives showed how thoughtless the call for an elected Senate is. Would elected senators serve until they reached age seventy-five like appointed senators? A senator who, once elected, would never have to face the voters again would escape democratic accountability. Or would senators stand for re-election when Parliament was dissolved, or, as one commentator suggested,[87] at provincial elections? Or would they serve ten- or six-year fixed terms. No one seemed to know or know how to decide.

The populists demand elections but how, when, where (should the provinces be divided into senatorial ridings?) they do not know. Logic might suggest a Senate elected exactly as the House of Commons is, finally laying bare the absurdity of the project.

The plethora of ideas for Senate reform, running as far as a suggestion that senators might be selected rather like juries, by lot,[88] demonstrates the earnest frivolity of Senate reform. If the Senate were failing to serve a compelling purpose, there would be some consensus on what should be done with it.

In a Fix Again

Harper's first step, the bill to limit the term of newly appointed senators to eight years, is a stopgap measure, a gesture towards reform,
arguably unconstitutional and introduced to make the patronage plum
look less rich. So long as senators are appointed, it can only make the
Senate worse. Tenure to age seventy-five has assured that senators,
however much party favourites on appointment, can become relatively
independent with time. They need not concern themselves with elections, nor need they concern themselves with the government, which
gives up its power over them in appointing them. Limiting Senators'
terms makes them party dependents, hoping for reappointment, some
other patronage, or a nomination.

Eight-year terms would make possible the appointment of the whole
Senate by a prime minister serving eight years, and more than half of
it in the life of one Parliament. The measure cannot be excused by the
argument that senators will effectively be elected by the time it comes
into effect, because that may not be the case, and how they may be
elected and how an elected Senate may work is still unknown. It could
be difficult to reverse, even if Harper's messing about is swept aside.

The provision to limit senators to one eight-year term, which was
added to the bill when it was reintroduced in the Second Session of
the Thirty-ninth Parliament, on the one hand shows how little the government had thought through the measure. On the other, it does not
effectively counter the effect of limited terms on the independence of
senators. Unless senators are to be so many Cincinnati returning to
their farms after eight years of service, they will still be party players
worrying about their careers and what the party can do for them and
they should do for it. Senators appointed to serve to age seventy-five,
however loyal they may remain to their party, need no longer jockey for
position or cultivate the current leader.

Moreover, a provision intended to deal with the charge that, hoping
for reappointment, senators with eight-year terms would be beholden
to the government that could reappoint them would apply to elected
senators. Term limits bring another American institution into our politics where it has no place. Barring people from standing for re-election
is essentially undemocratic. It does not simply affect the individual
barred from running, it denies the voters the right to choose the person
who may be their favourite.

And if the balance of legal opinion was that simply limiting the term of senators was within Ottawa's constitutional powers, altering eligibility for appointment by excluding a class of people who have already served a term in the Senate is likely not within Ottawa's constitutional powers.

Stéphane Dion wanted twelve-year terms, and the Senate Legal and Constitutional Affairs Committee wanted fifteen-year terms. Why not to age seventy-five?

How Provincial!

Some have suggested that provincial governments should appoint senators. Again the question arises, for what term? Or should provincially appointed senators serve at the pleasure of the provincial governments, acting as their delegates and following their instructions? As they are envisaged by some as a means of supervision of Ottawa by the provincial governments, logically they should. Such an idea could only appeal to premiers. The provincial governments are powerful enough. The constitution distributes powers between the dominion and provincial governments, and the latter have no more business interfering in the government of Canada than Ottawa has interfering in the government of the provinces.

Regional representation in the Senate was never intended to give the provinces, in the sense of provincial governments, power in Ottawa. If it had been, the provinces would have appointed the senators from Confederation. At the time, United States senators were chosen by the state legislatures. But when Confederation was devised, the provinces did not exist. New Brunswick and Nova Scotia were autonomous, self-governing colonies legally and politically very different from the provinces created by Confederation. The Province of Canada was another self-governing colony, and Quebec and Ontario did not exist. The allocation of Senate seats had nothing to do with the interests of provincial governments that did not exist. It was geographically dispersed interests and perspectives that were to be reflected in the Senate. If the provinces are to appoint senators to supervise the national government, the legislative councils should be revived and Ottawa appoint their members to supervise provincial governments in the national interest.

Why should regions or provinces have representation greater than their population indicates in the national government? Canada's answer to accommodating the diverse interests of its regions is federalism. Each province has a government of its own, with large powers to govern as local interests and customs dictate. At the national level we must have enough trust in each other to support a common government or the country fails. It was one of the ends of Confederation to achieve representation by population. As Ontario's population outstripped Quebec's, the equal representation of Canada East and Canada West legislated by the Act of Union became intolerable. To elect an effective Senate rejecting representation by population would be to reject one of the principles of Confederation.

Of course those principles have always been pragmatically compromised. Prince Edward Island's four seats in the House of Commons, four times as many as its population could justify, is one compromise. But it is a small compromise for a small province. If there is unhappiness with representation by population sufficient to justify its being abandoned in an effective elected Senate, it should be abandoned for the House of Commons. But it will not be, because people would rightly think it unfair. What Senate reformers want to do is to sneak it in by the back door, where it would be as rightly objectionable as in the Commons if it were effective, and simply disruptive and distracting if it were not.

Phoney Elections

While the Meech Lake Accord, which provided for the nomination of senators by provincial government, awaited ratification, Brian Mulroney appointed the late Stan Waters to the Senate eight months after he won a phoney election for a vacant seat staged by the Alberta government in October 1989. The election legislation was flagrantly unconstitutional. Only about 40 per cent of the electorate voted in an election timed to coincide with the municipal elections. On its own, the vote would, no doubt, have been lower. Reform – Waters's party – the PCs, and the Liberals ran candidates, but the New Democrats boycotted the election. Mulroney was trying to soothe a restless West. Much good it did him.

Further illegal elections were held in Alberta in 1998 and 2004. The Liberals joined the New Democrats in boycotting them. Jean Chrétien filled the two vacancies in 1998 shortly before the vote. For 2004 the legislation was amended to allow the election of 'nominees' for anticipated vacancies in the Senate. Chrétien and Martin went ahead and appointed their own choices anyway.

The Reform Party put up the winning candidates in 1998, but three of the winners in 2004, when the election took place with the provincial

general election, were put up by the provincial Progressive Conservatives. The participation of a provincial party in an election ostensibly
for a national position confirmed the confusion inherent in Alberta's
Senate shenanigans. Election legislation generally bars provincial parties from supporting candidates in national elections, and vice versa.
The participation of a provincial party in a Senate election under provincial law implies the theory of an elected Senate as an instrument of
provincial government control over the national government. On that
logic each province should decide its own way of choosing senators.

And on the logic that justifies Alberta's phoney Senate elections
Ottawa would be as well entitled to push for the revival of provincial
legislative councils by organizing elections for legislative councillors in
each province. The idea is absurd. So are Alberta's Senate elections. If
upper houses, even elected, for the provinces seem absurd, why does
an elected Senate not seem absurd? In part just because the Senate is
there, but largely because the West placed its hopes in an elected Senate. In the future, the West's strength will be in the House of Commons.

The winners in Alberta's Senate elections become 'nominees' waiting
for appointment by a sympathetic government in case of a vacancy perhaps years off. They 'serve' six-year terms as nominees for a position
that may have an eight-year term or be to age seventy-five. The voters
are asked to choose someone to represent them fourteen years or more
later or never.

The fortuitous resignation of Liberal Senator Dan Hays seven years
early gave Harper a chance to appoint sixty-nine-year-old Bert Brown,
who had garnered the most votes in Alberta's pseudo-elections in 1998
and 2004. Brown's appointment was hailed by champions of an elected
Senate, and even Westerners who have cooled to the idea but admired
Brown's doughty championing of it over twenty years. To the question
whether he was qualified for the job the ready answer was that plenty
of duds had been appointed to the Senate without a vote to their name.
A traditional joke has it that an obsession with Senate reform was a sign
of dementia.[89] In Brown's case it was his one qualification for the job.
Those who voted for him were voting for an elected Senate. They were
not deciding who would make the best senator.

A Parliamentary Lie

To proceed with his Senate agenda Stephen Harper asked Parliament to lie. The Senate Appointment Consultations Act, introduced in
December 2008, was promoted as providing for elections to the Senate

but, because that would require an amendment to the constitution, it pretended merely to provide for consultations with the voters, what elections are often called. Except when donning the robes of hired constitutional lawyers, everyone talked of the bill as providing for an elected Senate.[90] The provincial legislation in Alberta and Saskatchewan speaks frankly of elections, but they are in theory only electing nominees to the Senate. Its supporters believed that in practice the availability and the results of the 'consultations' would compel appointments. If they were right, the bill was flagrantly unconstitutional.

The act provided for 'consultations' at the time of national or provincial general elections. Senate vacancies would have accumulated until a general election. Unlike the legislation in Alberta and Saskatchewan, under Harper's bill the winners at the polls would not have been nominees waiting for a vacancy, They were to be immediately summoned to the Senate. Or not. There was no provision for by-elections. All Ontario being called out to vote for one senator must have been too much, even for the fanatics of reform. But the prospect was that there would always be several vacancies in the Senate occurring randomly, depending on terms, sickness, death, and retirement, and the sequence of general elections. The authority of the Senate would rightly have been sapped. As it was, Harper allowed eighteen vacancies to accumulate while figuring out what to do, despite the best efforts of the Liberals to fill the Senate up.

The consultations were to be by STV, whose follies I describe in chapter 4. For the Senate these follies will have been compounded by the likely fluctuations in the number of seats in play. With the system in full swing, as many as ten seats might have been open in Ontario, while at other times in other provinces there might have been none or only one. Under STV the number of seats open makes a great difference to the result, and the more seats open the more grotesquely complicated the ballot. These factors could be manipulated for political purposes.

Senate elections held at the same time as a national general election could be lost in the general election, with voters scarcely knowing what they were doing when faced with a complicated Senate ballot after casting a simple vote for their MP. Or Senate races could become a distraction from the general vote. When Senate elections were held with provincial general elections, provincial issues and feelings could prejudice a vote for a seat in the national parliament dealing with national issues.

It is no answer to say that Americans vote regularly for a president, a senator, a representative, a governor, and several state and local lawmakers and officials. American elections do no work well, and the extraordinary advantage of incumbency is stark evidence of that.

On Second Thoughts

Having let the Senate Appointments Consultation Act die on the order paper in two sessions of Parliament, the Harper government introduced a new Senatorial Selection Act in April 2010. It scraps the provisions for nationally run STV Senate elections and hands Senate elections over to the provinces, or even municipalities should a province choose to hold Senate elections with municipal elections. The consultation bills were carefully drafted to avoid the word *election*, but the new bill boldly provides for elections while pretending that only nominees, who 'should' be appointed to the Senate, will be elected. If a province holds election, the bill says, 'Senators to be appointed for a province ... *should* be chosen from a list of Senate nominees submitted by the government of the province' (my emphasis).

The provinces, and presumably provincial parties, are given a hand in the national government. Only on the basis that it has no legal force could this be constitutional.

Having seen the inability of Democracy Watch to understand the fixed election date legislation, we should be leery of legislation for elections that only *should*, that is, *ex hypothesi*, not a legally enforceable 'should,' result in the winner taking a seat in the Senate.

The bill opens up the prospect of a Senate made up of old appointees serving to age seventy-five or the end of an eight-year term, 'nominees' elected at various times and under various rules for single eight-year terms, and new appointees from provinces that will not hold elections. Enthusiasts for an elected Senate may hope that pressure will build on all provinces to hold elections, but it is as likely that some provinces will retreat from the mess.

However Senate elections might work, the makeup of the Senate could drift far from the makeup of the Commons and from current political feeling in the country. A new government could face a Senate in which the balance of power was held by senators elected at the time of provincial elections seven years before.

Harper's Game

Though both in the Reform Party and at the National Citizens Coalition Harper parroted the triple-E line, he never seemed a zealot. The

Conservative Party includes zealots, one-time zealots having doubts, an indifferent majority, and opponents. Harper's promotion of an elected Senate is partly the inertia of an old commitment and partly cynical politics. As Tony Blair gave the appearance of activity while scarcely straying from the course set by Margaret Thatcher by reforming the House of Lords in his first government, Harper, while following a Liberal course, pretends a new way of doing things with righteously hyped 'democratic reform.' His appointment of Michel Fortier to the Senate and the Cabinet as he was sworn in was an embarrassment that fussing about an elected Senate might put behind him.

Harper rudely threatened the Senate when it raised reasonable questions about his stabs at Senate reform and threatened an election on the issue, posing as the righteous democrat[91] while plainly never having thought through the issues and refusing to debate them. The government was clearly floundering in taking over six months between introducing the bill to limit Senate terms to eight years and the bill for 'consultations,' but Harper demanded that both bills be marched smartly to royal assent. Yet, for all his bluster, he did not make his 'consultations' bill, introduced in the Commons, a priority.[92] As his third try at Senate elections is a radical rewrite, he certainly did not know what he wanted, beyond a gesture on the order paper.

British Columbia and Ontario lean towards abolition, as do Manitoba and Saskatchewan, depending on who is in power. Quebec's National Assembly unanimously voted against any change without its approval, for which it would have a price.

Meech Lake and Charlottetown had the support of every government in Canada and all the federalist parties except for Reform, which, prior to its 1993 breakthrough, campaigned against Charlottetown. Rubbish though they were, they were not partisan political gambits. As with everything he does, Harper seeks electoral advantage from his Senate moves, though even his bright sparks can see that an election about Senate reform is not appealing. The issue was completely ignored in both the 2006 and 2008 elections. People may tell pollsters they are in favour of it, but they are not going to vote for a government they are otherwise leery of on that issue. Ask people nicely and they will also tell pollsters they favour abolition of the Senate.

If Harper proceeds with elections, he faces two insurmountable problems. It will be a generation before all the appointed senators are retired or dead. Pressure might be brought to force them to resign, but some will withstand it and with some popular sympathy. The Senate will be

a mixed elected and appointed body. The appointed senators w
more experience and be above the political grind. How such a
might conduct itself and what respect it might have we cannot te.

More seriously, Harper cannot change the distribution of Se
seats. As it is, British Columbia and Alberta, with six senators each,
the most under-represented provinces in relation to their populatioi
and it will only get worse. Their strength is increasing in the Common:
They have only 11 per cent of the Senate but over 20 per cent of the
Commons. By pressing forward with a reform intended to give the
West more strength, Harper risks weakening it.

However Harper may proceed, he is attempting a radical recasting of
the constitution as casual housekeeping. Proponents of appointing senators after what must be legally void elections think it is wonderfully
clever and simple. But if it is treated seriously, it will have a devastating
effect on government, and if the phoneyness of the elections is properly
appreciated by the voters, it will bring all elections into disrepute and
confuse and degrade democracy.

And however his game may play out, the one thing certain is that
Harper himself will never face an effective, elected Senate. By the time
anything like that exists, he will be out of office, an elder statesmen
remembered for little more than being the father of an elected Senate.
And while he messes around, only Conservatives are likely to be 'elected' in Alberta, the Conservative heartland, or Saskatchewan, where the
NDP is unlikely to field a candidate.

It may be argued that the flaws of Harper's scheme do not condemn
the project of an elected Senate. But other schemes will have other
flaws, and the flaws indicate that the proponents of an elected Senate
do not know what they are doing.

Business as Usual or Abolition

Getting nowhere with his lame and inept reform bills and with Mul-
roney-era senators disappearing faster than Liberals, Harper finally
caved and appointed eighteen senators, rather questionably while Parliament was prorogued in December 2008. His choices were unremark-
able, though apart from the celebrities, Nancy Greene, Mike Duffy, and
Pamela Wallin, rather less distinguished or experienced than usual.
Whether better prospects were reluctant to serve, given the commitment of many in his party to an elected Senate, or the stipulations
exacted for support for term limits and elections, or Harper was simply

propensity for appointing safe nonentities, the future for
folinted, and to be appointed as Harper seeks a majority in the
th has been unable to achieve in the Commons, is as obscure as
Se of Senate reform. The term limit legislation as reintroduced
econd Session of the Fortieth Parliament provides that the new
ntees will serve until eight years after the act comes into force.
are pledged to support the legislation but not to resign in eight
rs. And what is a pledge on Harper's team? Pamela Wallin has said
e will stand down and run for election whenever Saskatchewan gets
around to staging an election under legislation passed in May 2009 by
the Saskatchewan Party government after Lorne Calvert's NDP, who
favoured abolition, were defeated. By the time you read this, we shall
have seen whether Saskatchewan wants to spend a million dollars to
see our Pam elected for what might still be an indefinite term.

While Harper's legislation was languishing, the NDP, true to its
CCF roots, proposed a referendum on abolishing the Senate. Harper
responded positively,[93] but the NDP motion got nowhere as some
weighed in to say other options should be on a ballot and the election
the referendum was to coincide with awaited the fates.

Harper's further nine appointments in August 2009 produced the
usual carping and sneering, and a study by NDP MP Peter Stoffer cal-
culating that his twenty-seven appointments would cost taxpayers
$177 million in salaries, benefits, and expenses if they all served to age
seventy-five. As an argument for the NDP's historic position of abolition this carries some weight, but the cost of an elected Senate would be
several times that, and the NDP should be trumpeting that.

Harper and many others were caught in the position of saying the
Senate must be beefed up with elections and play a larger role in Parliament, or we could just do without it. If an elected Senate is so important, how could we think of abolishing it? If we can think of abolishing
it, why should we not just leave it in harmless peace?

Still Standing

Anxious journalists and political scientists fret that we live under an
elective dictatorship and need an effective upper house to restrain it.
But it is the job of the Commons to hold governments responsible and
to restrain them. No upper house, anywhere, ever thwarted popular
dictatorship. What the unreformed Senate can do, using its full powers, is restrain a government safe in the Commons but unpopular in

the country. Senators do not need to be elected to assume the role of champions of the people when the role is open. But the Commons is more likely to do its job if we do not look elsewhere, to a Senate, or the courts, to trammel government. An elected effective Senate would either encourage overconfident government, when it held sway in both houses, or make government irresponsible and ineffective when the houses were divided. If the Senate does not seem worth the money, best it were abolished like the legislative councils in the provinces. Its chief fault is that, so long as it exists, it is the subject of foolish dreams of reform. If it had never existed or had been abolished decades ago, would we be talking about it? Of course not.

13 Let It Be

To be against all proposed reforms of our political institutions is necessarily conservative in the basic sense of the word. But it is not my purpose in arguing for things as they are to make Canada safe for conservatives. Our institutions can be made to serve any politics – socialist, liberal, neo-con, green – if voters can be persuaded to support them. It is on the arguments over substance, not procedure, that our politics should focus.

The purpose of democracy is to let the people decide. Under our present institutions we do. We choose a government, hold it responsible, turf it out. With electoral reform and possibly an elected Senate that would end. The conflicts amongst us would be carried up and politicians would make deals beyond our control.

The purpose of government is to choose. With competing houses of Parliament, competing parties in government, MPs all wanting to do their own thing, tenured whether they worked together or not, waves of popular protest making law, politicians in and out as the voters' moods take them, government could no longer make choices. There would only be deals, and where there were not, old choices would become permanent because nothing new could be agreed upon.

Some of the reforms I attack in this book may be otiose, distracting at worst. Others would gravely damage our democratic government and make it ineffective and beyond the control of the people it should serve. Reform may be a passing fashion. Some reforms adopted may be dropped. But most reforms, once adopted, will create interests that will make their reversal well nigh impossible.

As long as we look to reform to remove our political discontents, we shall be distracted from squarely facing what is wrong with our politics. It is in understanding the rights and wrongs of what governments do, and what we need in those who do it – policies and people, the substantive issues of politics – that the way forward lies.

Notes

1 Throughout this book, examples taken from Ottawa apply equally to the provincial governments and vice versa. For 'House of Commons' read 'legislative assembly.' Despite first steps towards reform, the basis of government in Ottawa and the provincial capitals remains the same, excepting the absence of upper houses in the provinces.

2 Sir Sandford Fleming, the railway engineer and promoter of standard time, called for electoral reform in 1892 in *An Appeal to the Canadian Institute on the Rectification of Parliament* (Toronto: Copp Clark, 1892).

3 Woodrow Wilson, *Congressional Government: A Study in American Politics* (Boston: Houghton Mifflin, 1885).

4 Ontario, Legislative Assembly, *Debates and Proceedings* (12 Dec. 2005), p. 1607 (Gilles Bisson, MLA).

5 Ontario, Legislative Assembly, *Debates and Proceedings* (1 June 2004), p. 2461 (Dalton McGuinty, MLA).

6 House of Assembly Act 2004, sec. 3.1. The legislation speaks only of a premier who resigns as leader of the governing party, not thinking of a leader ousted by the party, or dead or incapacitated or ousted by a caucus rebellion without resigning as leader, implicitly adopting parties as part of the constitution rather than simply arrangements to make the constitution work. The provision that the premier must advise the lieutenant governor to dissolve the assembly, regardless of what he or she may think, to give what may be insincere or dishonest advice, is a grotesque corruption of the constitution only possible from wilful refusal to understand it.

7 Elections Alberta, *The Report on the March 3, 2008 Provincial General Election of the Twenty-Seventh Legislative Assembly* (Edmonton: Chief Electoral Office, 2008), 67–8.

8 Murray Campbell, 'Saddle Up, the Wild West of Pre-Writ Will Be a Ride,' *Globe and Mail*, 24 June 2006.

9 Murray Campbell, 'Only 843 Days for the Liberals to Stay on Message,' *Globe and Mail*, 13 June 2005.
10 British Columbia, Legislative Assembly, *Debates and Proceedings* (21 Aug. 2001), p. 677 (Geoff Plant, MLA).
11 Brian Laghi, 'Prepare for Vote, PM Says,' *Globe and Mail*, 20 Dec. 2006.
12 Adrian Humphreys and Juliet O'Neill, 'Harper, Dion Swap Threats over Election,' *National Post*, 20 Aug. 2008.
13 Tom Flanagan, 'It's Time for Conservative Minority Brinkmanship,' *Globe and Mail*, 1 Aug. 2007.
14 'Much as he might like an early race, election dates are now fixed by legislation and he can't just ask the Governor-General to dissolve Parliament. The opposition must pass a no-confidence vote, and that just got a lot less likely.' Tom Flanagan, 'Thou Shalt Not Lean Too Far to the Right,' *Globe and Mail*, 22 Sept. 2007.
15 Brian Laghi and Bill Curry, 'Harper's Election Ultimatum,' *Globe and Mail*, 4 Oct. 2007.
16 Bea Vongdouangchanh, 'PM "Has Every Right" to ask GG to Dissolve Parliament on Anti-Crime Bill: Tory Senator,' *Hill Times*, 25 Feb. 2008; Gloria Galloway, 'Senate's Crime Bill Vote Unlikely to Spark Election,' *Globe and Mail*, 26 Feb. 2008.
17 Standing Senate Committee on Legal and Constitutional Affairs, Proceedings, 6 Dec. 2006.
18 Don Martin, 'Harper May Have to Break His Own Election Law,' *National Post*, 10 Apr. 2008.
19 Norman Spector, 'The Haunting of Harper: Fixed Dates, Public Inquiry,' *Globe and Mail*, 1 Jan. 2008.
20 Democracy Watch, 'Democracy Watch Federal Court of Appeal ruling means Harper Conservatives broke their 2006 election promise to fix election dates,' news release, 26 May 2010.
21 'Mr McGuinty could walk down the hall today or the day after this legislation comes into effect and ask the Lieutenant Governor to dissolve Parliament, and the Lieutenant Governor would be obligated to do so, because that's in our Constitution.' Ontario, Legislative Assembly, *Debates and Proceedings* (12 Dec. 2005), p. 1604 (Norman W. Sterling, MLA).
22 The Constitution Act, 1982, para. 41(a).
23 Bill 54, Fixed Dates for Elections Act (June 7, 2007 Commencement), 2004, 1st sess., 38th Legislature Ontario, 2004.
24 James R. Robertson, Bill C-16: An Act to Amend the Canada Elections Act, 9–10.
25 '"Jamaica" Coalition Gains Support in Germany,' Angus Reid Global Monitor, 28 Sept. 2005.

26 'Germans Wary of Grand Coalition Talks,' Angus Reid Global Monitor, 4 Oct. 2005, http://www.angus-reid.com.

27 Patrick Saint-Paul, 'Les Bavarois de la CDU dénoncent la campagne "au valium" de Merkel,' Le Figaro, 17 Sept 2009.

28 'Grün für Merkel,' Financial Times Deutschland, 21 Sept. 2009.

29 Bertrand Benoit, 'Broken Voting System Opens Way for Divine Intervention,' Financial Times, 1 Sept. 2009.

30 Joseph A. Schumpeter, Capitalism, Socialism and Democracy, 6th ed. (London: Counterpoint Unwin Paperbacks, 1987), 272.

31 Karl R. Popper, The Open Society and Its Enemies (New York: Harper Torchbooks, 1963), vol. 1, chap. 7; Popper, 'The Open Society and Its Enemies Revisited,' Economist, 23 Apr. 1988.

32 Michael Pinto-Duschinsky, 'Sending the Rascals Packing,' Times Literary Supplement, 25 Sept. 1998.

33 'Canadians Want Current Parliament to Work,' Angus Reid Global Monitor, 11 Apr. 2006.

34 'Harper Begins Tenure at 54%,' Angus Reid Global Monitor, 16 Feb. 2006.

35 'Canadians Expect Better Government under Harper,' Angus Reid Global Monitor, 28 Feb. 2006.

36 Law Commission of Canada, Voting Counts: Electoral Reform for Canada (Ottawa: Law Commission of Canada, 2004).

37 Tom Flanagan, 'The Alternative Vote: An Electoral System for Canada,' in Making Every Vote Count, ed. Henry Milner (Peterborough, ON: Broadview, 1999), 85.

38 Kenneth J. Arrow, Social Choice and Individual Values (New Haven: Yale University Press, 1951), 59.

39 Leslie Sykes, Proportional Representation: Which System? (Leicester: Hornbeam, 1990), xii; Michael Dummett, Principles of Electoral Reform (Oxford: Oxford University Press, 1997), 91.

40 Gordon Gibson, 'Why Politicians Don't Like the STV,' Vancouver Sun, 14 Dec. 2004.

41 British Columbia Citizens' Assembly on Electoral Reform, Making Every Vote Count: The Case for Electoral Reform in British Columbia – Final Report (Victoria: British Columbia Citizens' Assembly on Electoral Reform, 2004).

42 British Columbia Citizens' Assembly on Electoral Reform, Making Every Vote Count: The Case for Electoral Reform in British Columbia – Technical Report (Victoria: British Columbia Citizens' Assembly on Electoral Reform, 2004).

43 Gordon Gibson, 'Democracy in America: One Day, They May Get It Right,' Globe and Mail, 28 Feb. 2007.

44 John Ibbitson, The Polite Revolution Perfecting the Canadian Dream (Toronto: McClelland & Stewart, 2005), 226.

45 British Columbia Citizens' Assembly, *Making Every Vote Count*, 1.

46 Doug Saunders, 'Kenny Urges Voting for Minor Parties,' *Globe and Mail*, 25 May 2007.

47 Walter Bagehot, *The English Constitution* (London: Fontana Library, 1963), 163.

48 F.A. Hermens, *Democracy or Anarchy? A Study of Proportional Representation* (Notre Dame: University of Notre Dame Press, 1941).

49 Adam Radwanski, 'Ontario May Lead Way in Electoral Reform,' *National Post*, 22 Dec. 2003.

50 Ontario, Legislative Assembly, Select Committee on Electoral Reform, *Report on Electoral Reform* (Toronto: Queen's Printer, 2005), 2, 52.

51 Ontario Citizens' Assembly on Electoral Reform, 'Be a Part of History in the Making,' backgrounder, 18 Aug. 2006.

52 The Ontario Citizens' Assembly Secretariat, *Democracy at Work: The Ontario Citizens' Assembly on Electoral Reform* (Toronto: Queen's Printer, 2007), 46.

53 Ibid., 67.

54 Ibid., 204.

55 Ibid., 150.

56 I treat the Christian Democratic Union and their Bavarian sister party, the Christian Social Union, as one for the purpose of this analysis. The CSU is effectively a regional branch of the CDU.

57 Commission on Boundary Differences and Voting Systems (Arbuthnott Commission), *Putting Citizens First: Boundaries, Voting and Representation in Scotland, Commission on Boundary Differences and Voting Systems* (Edinburgh: Stationery Office, 2006), 31–3, paras 4.12–4.17. The Arbuthnott Commission said, perhaps rightly, that the Greens were not to be blamed for campaigning to seek their best advantage from the voting system. But the system must be blamed if the Greens got half or more of their seats from voters who did not understand the consequences of their second vote, as appears to have happened. A change in the form of the ballot paper and voters understanding the system better perhaps led to the Greens falling from seven seats in 2003 to two in 2007. Stephen Herbert, Ross Burnside, Murray Earle, Tom Edwards, Tom Foley, Iain Mciver, 'Election 2007,' Scottish Parliament Information Centre briefing, 8 May 2007, 42, 46.

58 Citizens' Assembly on Electoral Reform, 'This Recommendation Carries Real Weight,' http://www.citizensassembly.gov.on.ca/en-ca/home%20page.html.

59 Vote for MMP, 'Pro-MMP Group Calls on John Tory to Affirm Respect for Citizen Democracy,' news release, 24 Sept. 2007.

60 'Ontario's Missed Opportunity,' *Globe and Mail*, 4 Oct. 2007.

61 Don Butler, '"Active Resistance" Starts to Greet MMP,' *National Post*, 21 Sept. 2007.

62 Vote for MMP, 'Toronto Star Wrong about Whether FPTP or MMP Leads to Political Chaos,' news release, 30 Sept. 2007.

63 Fred Cutler and Patrick Fournier, 'Why Ontarians Said No to MMP,' Globe and Mail, 25 Oct. 2007.

64 John Ibbitson 'Hung Parliament in Britain, Election Reform in Canada?' Globe and Mail, 7 May 2010.

65 Elizabeth Kuruvila and Jean-Denis Fréchette, 'Food Labelling – The Case of Dairy Products: Economic, Legislative and Trade Aspects' (Parliamentary Information and Research Service, 6 Oct. 2005).

66 House of Commons, Standing Committee on Agriculture and Agri-Food, Evidence, 17 Oct. 2005.

67 'Ethics, Responsibility, Accountability: An Action Plan for Democratic Reform,' Privy Council Office, 4 Feb. 2004.

68 In fact, the number of lines on a whip at Westminster does not indicate levels of 'freedom' or the greater or less indifference of the government to the vote, as Martin's whips purported to do. It indicates levels of urgency of attendance and voting.

69 'Ethics, Responsibility, Accountability,' 4.

70 Ibid.

71 Standing Orders of the House of Commons 110 and 111.

72 Patrick Monahan, 'Is It Jean Chrétien's Court?' Globe and Mail, 27 June 2003.

73 Rosalie Abella, 'The Civil Litigation Process under Siege: Roscoe Pound Redux,' Gazette [Law Society of Upper Canada] 28 (1994): 213. Speech given to the County of Carleton Law Association, 15 Nov. 1991.

74 Richard Blackwell, 'No Activist, Supreme Court Nominee Says,' Globe and Mail, 28 Feb. 2005.

75 Peter W. Hogg, 'Opening Remarks to Ad Hoc Committee on Supreme Court Appointment,' 27 Feb. 2006, http://canada.justice.gc.ca/eng/news-nouv/spe-disc/2006/doc_31772.html.

76 Jim Brown, 'MPs Clash over Vetting Supreme Court Candidates,' Toronto Star, 8 Aug. 2008.

77 Kirk Makin, 'Harper Blasted over Hasty Top-Court Nomination,' Globe and Mail, 6 Sept. 2008.

78 John Ward, 'Harper Nominates Nova Scotian to Supreme Court,' Globe and Mail, 5 Sept. 2008.

79 Alberta passed recall legislation in 1936 but repealed it in 1937 retroactive to the day it received royal assent, making it as if it had never been, after a petition was launched to unseat Premier William Aberhart.

80 In his 'Speech to the Electors of Bristol,' 3 Nov. 1774, Burke gave the classic statement on the role of an MP:

Your representative owes you, not his industry only, but his judgment; and he betrays, instead of serving you, if he sacrifices it to
your opinion … [A]uthoritative instructions; mandates issued, which
the member is bound blindly and implicitly to obey, to vote, and to
argue for, though contrary to the clearest conviction of his judgment
and conscience – these are things utterly unknown to the laws of
this land, and which arise from a fundamental mistake of the whole
order and tenor of our constitution.

See *The Writings and Speeches of Edmund Burke* (Oxford: Oxford University
Press, 1996), 3:69.

81 Peter McCormick, 'Recall of Elected Members,' *Canadian Parliamentary
Review* 17, no. 2 (Summer 1994): 4.

82 Martin, 'Harper May Have to Break His Own Election Law.'

83 W.L. Morton, 'Direct Legislation and the Origins of the Progressive Movement,' *Canadian Historical Review* 25 (September 1944): 281.

84 Justine Hunter, 'Elections BC Accused of Double Standard in HST Campaign,' *Globe and Mail*, 29 Apr. 2010.

85 Editorial, 'The Future of Canada's Senate,' *National Post*, 8 Nov. 2007.

86 Peter H. Russell, *Two Cheers for Minority Government: The Evolution of Parliamentary Democracy* (Toronto: Montgomery, 2008).

87 Lorne Gunter, 'Putting the Regions Back into the Senate,' *National Post*, 16
Mar. 2006.

88 Harry Koza, 'A Modest Proposal for Senate Reform: Jury Duty,' *Globe and
Mail*, 19 Nov. 2007. More earnestly, the third way think tank DEMOS pro-
posed a House of Lords selected by lot: Anthony Barnett and Peter Carly, *The
Athenian Option: Radical Reform of the House of Lords* (London: DEMOS, 1998).

89 Talk of Senate reform 'comes periodically like other forms of epidemic
and current fevers.' Canada, *House of Commons Debates* (2 Feb. 1926), p. 648
(Henri Bourassa, MP).

90 'The Tories unveiled bills in the last session on Senate term limits and a
process the would allow Canadian to *elect* Senators' (emphasis added).
Brian Laghi, 'Vote on Senate "Premature," PM Warned,' *Globe and Mail*, 7
Nov. 2007.

91 Allan Findlay, 'PM Threatens Election over Senate Reform,' *Calgary Sun*, 8
Sept. 2006.

92 Wilfred Moore, 'Harper Wants an Elected Senate, and Appointees Too,'
National Post, 27 Nov. 2008.

93 'Harper Would Back Plan for Referendum on Abolishing Senate,' *Globe and
Mail*, 6 Nov. 2007.

Index

The University of Toronto Centre for Public Management Monograph Series